An Illustrated History

The 29th Waffen-SS

Grenadier Division "Italienische Nr.1"

And Italians in other units of the Waffen-SS

Massimiliano Afiero

Schiffer Military
4880 Lower Valley Road Atglen, PA 19310

Originally published as *Italiani nella Waffen-SS* by Associazione Culturale Ritterkreuz © 2019 by Associazione Culturale Ritterkreuz, Afragola, Campania, Italy

Translated from the Italian by Ralph Riccio

Library of Congress Control Number: 2020952744

Type set in Minion Pro & Antique Olive Std

ISBN: 978-0-7643-6295-8

Printed in Serbia

Published by Schiffer Publishing, Ltd.

4880 Lower Valley Road

Atglen, PA 19310

Phone: (610) 593-1777; Fax: (610) 593-2002

E-mail: Info@schifferbooks.com

Web: www.schifferbooks.com

CONTENTS

Salò, February 1944: Mussolini inspecting a unit of Italian volunteers who have just returned from Greece

INTRODUCTION

The story of Italians who chose to fight in the ranks of the Waffen-SS is still unknown and still has to be written, perhaps because official historiography wishes to hide this aspect of Italy's recent past, as though it were something shameful to wash away into literary oblivion. It is convenient for everyone to continue to perpetuate the story that after September 8, 1943, with the signing of the armistice with the Allies, the Italians—all Italians—immediately ceased to be Fascists and allies of the Germans. Nothing is further from the truth. That fateful date of September 8 instead marked the beginning of a civil war that wore on for almost two more years, which saw Italians fight against other Italians, and Italians who chose to continue the war alongside their German allies, fighting against Allied forces that had invaded Italy. It was a difficult and agonizing choice, in part justified by the terrible events of those years, a choice that is even to this day condemned by official historiography, which has always painted these "volunteers" as cruel assassins in the pay of the Germans. We do not pretend to sit in judgment, especially after the passage of so many years. Our intent, above all, has been to understand the reasons for that choice, through the direct testimony of several of the protagonists, not to justify but rather to tell their stories, and for the historical truth. Most of the Italians who chose voluntarily or who were forced by events to fight alongside the Germans did so above all because they had an attachment to their homeland, an ideal that is not widespread in today's culture and has almost been forgotten by the youth in these times. It was a choice of honor to distance themselves from the "betrayal" of the House of Savoy and by the Italian armed forces, to the detriment of the Germans. Many Italian soldiers continued to bear arms, desiring above all to continue to fight against the Allied armed forces. However, they continued to pay the consequences of September 8, having to show the Germans, who had been "betrayed," that they were still good soldiers and, above all, faithful comrades. Their actions under fire allowed them to demonstrate that, particularly by those Italians who ended up fighting in the various Waffen-SS divisions engaged in the main fronts of the war, from the Eastern Front to Normandy. After the battles on the Anzio and Nettuno fronts in the spring of 1944, the Italian SS units found themselves unfortunately embroiled in the terrible civil war that raged throughout the country, engaged in fighting against their own brothers, always however with the intention of continuing to serve their country. They often asked to be sent to the front lines, but it was not until close to the end of the war that some units fought against the Allies, with satisfactory results. At the end, following the defeat of the German armed forces, they also fell into oblivion, forced to hide and to forget their military service. Many paid for their choice with their lives. It is very difficult even today for historians to gather testimony from these soldiers, who are still fearful after so many years of being accused of crimes against the civilian populace. It is certain that there were those who were involved in criminal episodes, and they should rightly be condemned. Our historical research does not wish to and cannot justify or exalt certain episodes of Italy's recent past but aims only at studying and analyzing them with the utmost discipline and without any personal interpretations. It is admittedly a difficult task, but the results will, I hope, be worth the effort. I would like to thank all those who helped make this volume a reality, including all of the members of our association—Stefano Canavassi, Mauro Cardellini, Sergio Corbatti, Cesare Veronesi, Pierluigi Romeo di Colloredo Mels, Lorenzo Silvestri, Alessio Polignano, and Lorenzo Barzaghi, and in a special way all of the ex-combatants, some of whom are still alive and many of whom unfortunately have passed on, who have allowed us to publish their wartime experiences.

Massimiliano Afiero

CHAPTER I
ITALIAN VOLUNTEERS IN THE WAFFEN-SS

Assistant machine gun team leader of the 49th CCNN Assault Legion "San Marco" in the Balkans. *USSME*

Italian volunteers being directed by a German soldier toward a recruiting center. *Signal magazine*

Reichsführer-SS Heinrich Himmler

Enlistment of Italian soldiers in various Waffen-SS units began shortly after July 25, 1943, with the fall of Fascism and the removal of Benito Mussolini as head of the Italian government. In the midst of the disorder and the climate of confusion that permeated the entire country, many Italian soldiers decided to continue to fight alongside their German ally, especially members of the Milizia (Militia), who presented themselves voluntarily at German military headquarters. It was clear to everyone that the new Italian government, headed by Marshal Badoglio, was ready to betray Nazi Germany and shift over to the Allied side.

Reichsführer-SS Heinrich Himmler began to receive news from various sources, especially from abroad, concerning the influx of Italian soldiers to SS headquarters. For example, as early as July 28, 1943, many Italian Fascist Milizia soldiers in Zagreb had showed up at the local German headquarters, expressly requesting to be enlisted in the Waffen-SS. A few days later, there was news of similar episodes at German headquarters in the South Tyrol: there also, many members of the Milizia were volunteering at enlistment centers for ethnic German South Tyroleans, who, according to agreements reached between Hitler and Mussolini, could choose to enlist in German units. Despite the fact that official historiography has always spoken of Himmler's diffidence toward Italian volunteers and his conviction that Italians were not good fighters, the *Reichsführer-SS* quickly issued orders to accept the Italians. Surely Hitler did not have much love for the Italians, but after having taken in volunteers for the Waffen-SS from every corner of Europe and Asia, he certainly did not want to miss the opportunity to constitute SS units with members of the Fascist Milizia, who had quickly displayed their desire to continue on fighting against their longtime enemies.

Soldiers of an MVSN militia battalion during a ceremony

Bolzano, September 1943: Italian soldiers, captured by the Germans, on their way to a prison camp

Balkan front, September 1943: Italian soldiers who were left without orders or directives from their headquarters speak with German soldiers to decide their fate. After September 8, most Italian soldiers ended up in prison camps in Germany.

In the weeks that followed, reports of Italian soldiers who wished to continue fighting alongside the Germans multiplied, so on August 31, 1943, Himmler sent a secret message[1] to the various recruitment centers, in which he specified the behavior to follow with respect to the Italian volunteers, making a clear distinction: soldiers of the Regio Esercito (Italian Royal Army) were to be incorporated into the ranks of the Wehrmacht, while members of the Fascist Milizia would be integrated into the Waffen-SS.

September 8, 1943

On September 8, 1943, with the announcement of the armistice between the Badoglio government and the Allies, the Germans activated Plan Alaric, the invasion of Italy, and Plan Achse, the capture and disarmament of all Italian soldiers in Italy and abroad. German troops who were already on Italian territory and those who entered from the North met with little resistance; Italian units, lacking any adequate orders and left completely to themselves by higher headquarters, could do very little. Most soldiers, in Italy and those abroad, some 600,000 men, were thus disarmed by the Germans and transferred to Germany and Poland as prisoners. There was, of course, no lack of incidents and bloody encounters, especially in Yugoslavia and in Greece, where some units refused to turn over their weapons to the Germans and defended themselves to the last, victims not only of the ex-German ally but of the Italian high command and of the king as well (who fled disgracefully from Rome along with Badoglio to save their own skins), who had left them completely on their own without any guidance. In the midst of all of that chaos, as had already begun on the day after July 25, many units, aware of the "betrayal" by the king and the Italian government, decided to collaborate with the German forces. Italian military personnel from the Atlantic base at Bordeaux in France, the sailors at Danzig, MAS units located on the Black Sea, and many other units on various fronts reacted similarly. Some units were quickly integrated into German formations and sent to the front line. Particular attention was given to specialized personnel who were useful to the Germans for the continuation of the war. On September 15, the OKW issued a new order (Nr.005282/43g.), which reiterated the treatment to be accorded to Italian military personnel: "Let those who wish to fight keep their weapons and treat them well so as not to damage their honor as soldiers." Despite these directives by higher headquarters, many German commanders had their doubts about employment of Italian military personnel: generally speaking, they preferred to use them in police or antipartisan duties in Italy and abroad. Others proposed their use exclusively in Wehrmacht auxiliary units or in paramilitary formations such as Todt, the NSKK, and other such organizations.

Greece, October 1943: Italian volunteers integrated in a Luftwaffe flak battery during a swearing-in ceremony. The volunteers are wearing Luftwaffe tropical uniforms with insignia on the jacket lapels. *HK*

September 1943: Captured Italian soldiers being escorted by Leibstandarte grenadiers. *NA*

Italians in the Waffen-SS

The earliest enlistment of Italian volunteers into SS units occurred soon after September 8, even though in the weeks preceding that, some elements of the Milizia had enlisted in areas outside Italy. These soldiers were integrated into various SS formations as combat troops and not merely as auxiliaries (*Hiwis*). In addition, differing from the Italian volunteers who were later integrated into the Italian SS Legion, the Italian volunteers who were enlisted into Reichsdeutsche[2] divisions had their blood group tattooed under their left arm and were immediately granted the privilege of wearing the black insignia with the SS double runes on their uniforms. During that period, there were only three large Waffen-SS formations in Italy, the Leibstandarte, the Reichsführer assault brigade, and the SS-Karstwehr Bataillon.

At least three hundred Italian soldiers were enlisted in the 1.SS-Panzer-Division Leibstandarte SS Adolf Hitler[3] (LAH) immediately following September 8. The German commanders welcomed the presence of the Italians in their units, using them as drivers and mechanics to maintain the many vehicles of Italian origin that had been confiscated. Many of these volunteers later ended up in combat units when they went along with the Leibstandarte to the Ukraine in November 1943, participating in hard fighting against Soviet units. Some, such as Giuseppe Benedetti, were awarded the Iron Cross Second Class and the Wound Badge and promoted to *Unterscharführer* for having distinguished himself in combat in the Zhitomir area in the winter of 1943–44.[4] When the Leibstandarte units were transferred to the Istrian Peninsula to fight against Tito's partisan bands, many young Istrians and Friulians also enlisted in it. In March 1944, some fifty survivors agreed to return to Italy to be integrated into the Italian SS Legion. Initially transferred from the division's depot at Lichterfelde to Berlin, they were escorted on a train to Verona by SS-Oberschaführer Willy Detering. These Leibstandarte Adolf Hitler veterans from the Eastern Front were allowed the privilege of wearing the black tabs with the SS double runes, whereas the other members of the Italian SS wore red tabs. Among them was Unterscharführer Giuseppe Medda, who in September 1944 was seriously wounded and lost one of his legs while he tried to foil an attack against the Italian SS barracks in Pinerolo.

Another Italian volunteer in the Leibstandarte was Ferdinando Gandini. His experience with the war began as far back as June 1941, at the age of fifteen and a half, when he enlisted in the "M" battalions, like so many other youths in love with their country. Wounded in Albania and still convalescing at his home in Milan, on July 25, 1943, he reported to his military district, where a number of Fascists had taken refuge. There he joined up with his fellow soldiers, was ordered to put on his rank insignia, and was given travel papers to go to the camp at Trastevere in Rome. A few days later, the camp was moved to the ancient baths of Caracalla. On September

Columns of Italian prisoners escorted by soldiers of the Leibstandarte in an Italian city, September 1943. *NA*

8, between 1730 and 1800, the announcement from Badoglio arrived. Like many others, he did not wish to surrender to or betray the German ally, so he decided to return to Milan, where he arrived on September 14. His introduction to the Leibstandarte Adolf Hitler happened quite by accident: because of the flight and the roundup of his former comrades, Gandini went out into the street and, with his rank insignia and decorations in hand, stopped the first German truck that happened to be driving along Via Spallanzani, asking them to take him along with them. The Germans took him aboard and drove him to the Hotel Diana, where the German headquarters was located. After a discussion with the interpreter and hiding his age (he was seventeen years old), he was enlisted into SS-Pz.Gren.Rgt.1 LAH. He first went to Istria with the SS division, where he fought against Tito's partisan bands, and then went to the Eastern Front, where he took part in the terrible fighting during the relief operation for the Korsun-Cherkassy pocket between January and February 1944. Still with the division, he participated in the fighting at Normandy and later in the Ardennes counteroffensive, during which he was wounded by an exploding mine. Following about three months of convalescence in a military hospital, he once again joined up with the division south of Vienna, to take part in the last of the fighting. In the meantime, he had been promoted to the rank of *SS-Sturmmann* and awarded the Iron Cross Second Class. With the end of the war, he managed to return to Italy.[5]

A PzKpfw.IV of the Leibstandarte Adolf Hitler in Piazza Duomo in Milan, September 1943

With regard to other Italian volunteers in the Leibstandarte, at least a hundred or so continued to fight with the division until the end of the war, while others were in part transferred in the spring of 1944 to 12.SS-Panzer-Division Hitlerjugend and fought in Normandy, while others were assigned to s.SS-Panzer-Abteilung 501, the I.SS-Panzer-Korps heavy tank battalion. In a unit report dated September 5, 1944, twenty-one Italian volunteers were listed as having been killed or missing during the fighting in Normandy.[6] Of the group of Italian volunteers in Hitlerjugend, only about a dozen survivors returned to Italy in January 1945.

In the Sturmbrigade, later the 16.SS-Panzergrenadier-Division Reichsführer-SS, which operated on the Italian front and was involved in many of the worst massacres of civilians in Italy (Marzabotto and Sant'Anna di Stazzema), there were about a hundred Italians in the ranks, mainly in noncombat units, services, and administrative duties.[7] Other Italians ended up in the division when the unit was transferred to the Hungarian front in 1945, coming from schools, other training camps, and even prison camps.

Panzers of the Leibstandarte in Milan, 1943

Units of the SS-Karstwehr Bataillon arrived in Italy shortly after September 8, crossing through the Thörl-Maglern Pass and soon arriving at Tarvisio. There, the small Italian garrison surrendered without a fight. The same occurred at Camporosso and Boscoverde, while at Ugovizza the Italian garrison refused to lay down their arms; a brief but sharp fight ensued, which in the end saw the Karstjäger Division prevail, after having suffered about ten killed. During the early days of the unit's stay in Italy, several dozen Italians were recruited to be used as interpreters and guides. Among them

Hitlerjugend soldiers in Normandy

Italian and German prisoners captured in Normandy by the Allies

Assault guns of the Sturmbrigade Reichsführer-SS in Rome

A patrol of the SS-Karstwehr Bataillon in action

was Captain Giuseppe Occelli of the alpine troops. These early "enlistees" were not officially enrolled in the SS and continued to wear the Italian uniform. When operations to disarm Italian units were terminated, the battalion was transferred to Val Canale, where activity by Communist partisan bands was more intense. From there, the SS mountain troop unit was transferred to the Istrian Peninsula, where new Italian, Slovene, and Croat volunteers were recruited.

The Situation outside Italy

About a hundred Italian volunteers, belonging to units that were located in France following September 8, were enlisted in the 17.SS-Panzergrenadier-Division Götz von Berlichingen thanks to propaganda activity carried out by the military chaplain Padre Eusebio. The division, commanded by SS-Oberführer Werner Ostendorff, was being constituted in central France, in the region south of the Loire, with its divisional headquarters at Thouars, in the Deux-Sèvres Departement. It was thus that many Italians found themselves wearing an SS uniform fighting against the Allies in Normandy in June 1944. The division lost half of its manpower during the fighting: the Italian volunteers, around a hundred, returned to Italy and were integrated into the Italian SS Legion, and to the Folgore parachute regiment. As witness to the presence of Italians in the 17.SS, a telegram was sent to Mussolini in February 1945 that started, "Today more than yesterday the Italian volunteers serving in the SS Götz von Berlichingen Division reaffirm their unwavering faith in you. Since October 1943, the SS volunteers facing the invasion on French soil have known how to show with their blood their attachment to the Fascist cause, and many have fallen, but those who are still alive

SS-Karstwehr Bataillon mountain troopers engaged in an antipartisan operation. *Corbatti*

Grenadiers of 17.SS-GvB in Normandy, 1944

An Italian volunteer, wearing an arm band, and soldiers of the SS-Polizei-Division in Greece

will continue to march on the path shown to them by the dead: Italy. *Signed*: Raffaele Acurzio." At that time, the division was engaged in fighting on the Lorraine front and was withdrawing to the Palatinate under pressure from American troops.

In Greece, the 4.SS-Polizei Panzergrenadier Division also enlisted several hundred Italians from the Milizia and the army in the area around Volos. Initially, the volunteers continued to wear the Italian uniform and were assigned mainly to the division's support units. All the drivers of the 2nd Medical Company of the Polizei were Italian. Milizia personnel were instead assigned to combat units: an entire company of Blackshirts (around 180 men) designated the Compagnia Camicie Nere "L'Aquila" operated in the division's 7.SS-Panzergrenadier Regiment until autumn of 1944. An entire artillery group was also organized manned by Blackshirts.

In Yugoslavia, about a hundred Italians were attached to the 7.SS-Freiwillingen-Gebirgs-Division Prinz Eugen. The division was involved in disarming the Italian forces in Yugoslavia, and there were many instances of firefights, with losses on both sides. Many Italian soldiers and officers were summarily executed because they would not surrender their weapons to the Germans. The bloodiest episodes occurred in Spalato, Metkovic, Ragusa, and Trebinje. Once the fighting was over, an entire battalion of Italian engineers was integrated into the engineer elements of 7.SS Prinz Eugen. Other Italian soldiers served in the headquarters companies of the division's two regiments, as well as in the veterinary company.

About a hundred other Italians from the Lombardia Division, particularly those from a tank battalion attached to that division, ended up in *11.SS-Freiwilligen Panzergrenadier Division Nordland*. In September 1943, the division was deployed in Croatia as part of Felix Steiner's III.SS-Pz.Korps, completing training of new recruits prior to assignment to the Eastern Front. In December 1943, when Nordland was transferred to the Leningrad front, the Italian volunteers were transferred to Italy to be integrated into the Italian SS Legion.

There were about a hundred Italian volunteers in Lèon Degrelle's Wallonien Brigade, later a division. These were mostly men of Italian descent who were born in Belgium or Italians who were in Belgium for work. In December 1944, about fifty of them, along with about a dozen Spanish volunteers who were former soldiers in the Division Azul, requested to be transferred to Italy to serve in the Italian SS Legion. Degrelle consented, and in January 1945 the Italo-Spanish group arrived the Alois Thaler training battalion at Rodengo-Saiano.

Polizei soldiers in Greece, 1943

Soldiers of the SS-Polizei-Division chatting with Greek civilians, 1943

September 1943, Balkan front: Italian soldiers captured and collected by units of the SS Prinz Eugen division, prior to their transfer to prison camps in Germany

Another hundred or so Italian volunteers assigned to the Italian SS Legion who had been sent to Prague for a specialized course for *Panzergrenadiers*, due to the turn of events, were assigned to an emergency unit—as often happened by that time in the war—attached to 10.SS-Panzer-Division Frundsberg. Most of them were lost in combat on the Oder front in February 1945.

A great many other Italians, coming from other specialty schools and even from prison camps ultimately fought in various German units on the Hungarian front, in particular in the 18.SS-Panzergrenadier-Division Horst Wessel; the testimony of veterans confirms the presence of Italian soldiers in the defense of Budapest between December 1944 and February 1945. The names of the units to which they were attached are not known, however.

There were several Italian volunteers in the SS Charlemagne Brigade, later upgraded to a division in February 1945, as confirmed by the testimony of some veterans. SS-Ustuf. Paul Pignard-Berthet, a platoon leader in the 1st Company who was wounded in Galicia and subsequently was the commander of the Stammkompanie, the depot company formed of Frenchmen, distinctly remembers one Italian who had previously fought in Africa and had several tattoos on his body. Naturally, in the French SS formation there were many Frenchmen of Italian origin, as were Fernand Costamagna and many others.

Several dozen Italians also served in the renowned 36.Waffen-Grenadier Division der SS, also known as the Dirlewanger Brigade (from the name of its commander, SS-Brigadeführer Oskar Dirlewanger). The Dirlewanger was a Waffen-SS disciplinary unit in which many Italians who had been detained in the Danzig-Matkau prison camp ended up, after having previously deserted the Italian SS Legion.

A group of German grenadiers, armed with a *Panzerfaust* and small arms, on the Silesian front, February 1945

German grenadiers and assault guns during the fighting on the Eastern Front

Tank hunter-killers armed with the *Panzerfaust*

It is probable that several Italians fought in the 38.SS-Panzergrenadier-Division Nibelungen, which in the final days of the war was employed in southern Bavaria against American units. This was as witnessed by an Italian veteran (S.T.), who after September 8 found himself in Germany and soon thereafter was assigned to work in an underground aircraft factory south of Munich. Between March and April 1945, the workers at the factory, lacking raw materials, following rudimentary training on how to use antitank weapons, were assigned to combat units and thrown against the American forces. The aforementioned S.T. well remembers how he, along with three other Italian ex-mechanics, ended up in a retreating SS unit (the members of the unit were wearing the double rune insignia) that fought south of Munich against an American armored unit. During the fighting, the Italians were obliged to defend themselves against the attacking American tanks by using *Panzerfäuste*. Their positions were, of course, overrun and our S.T. was miraculously saved, only because the air pressure caused by a massive explosion catapulted him among the branches of a tree, thus hiding him from the enemy. After regaining consciousness, he was able to avoid capture and, after much wandering about, was able to get across the border and return to Italy.

Finally, the Italian volunteers who served in Otto Skorzeny's special units should not be forgotten; Skorzeny commanded SS special units, the so-called SS-Jagdverbände, especially those in SS-Jagdverbände Südwest. That unit was divided into three subunits: Jagdeinsatz Italien, Jagdeinsatz Nordfrankreich and Jagdeinsatz Südfrankreich. Jagdeinsatz Italien consisted, naturally, of Italian volunteers under the command of Sturmbannführer Beck and the Italian *Hauptsturmführer* Martini, both former members of the Brandenburg.

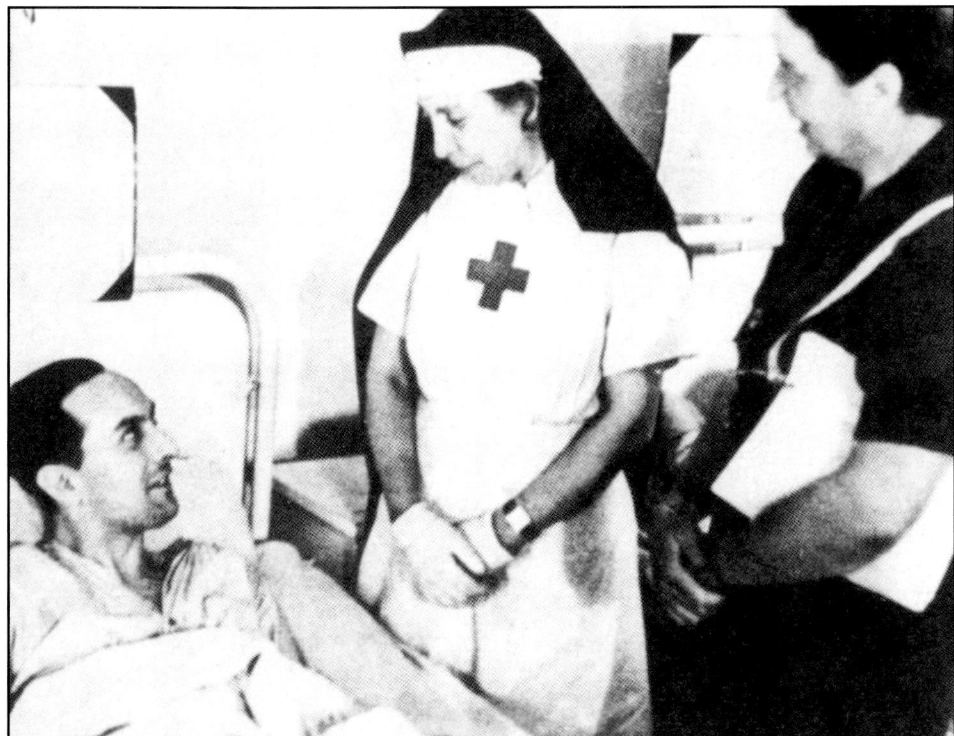

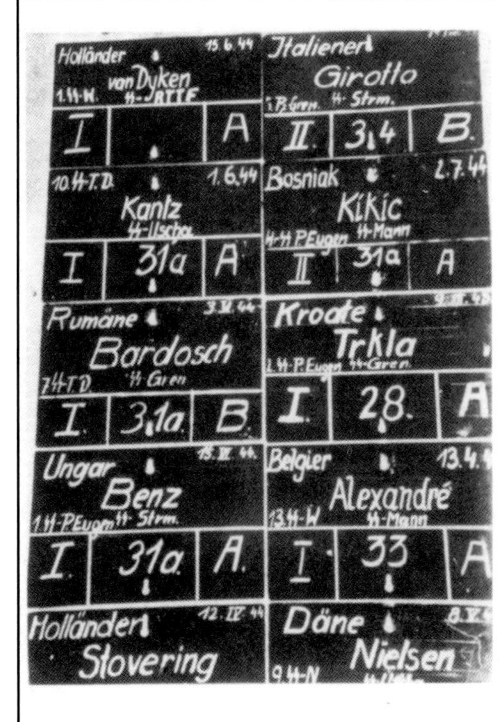

A famous photo that appeared in a period newspaper, showing an Italian volunteer, SS-Sturmmann Girotto, as can be seen in the photo on the right, a member of an SS unit, in a field hospital on the Eastern Front. *Ullstein*

Italian soldiers captured by the Germans following September 8. *Kuberski*

Otto Skorzeny

Chapter II

THE LEIBSTANDARTE ADOLF HITLER IN ITALY, SUMMER –AUTUMN 1943

SS-Oberfüher Teddy Wisch, commander of the Leibstandarte Adolf Hitler

Soldiers of the Leibstandarte Adolf Hitler with an MG42 machine gun defending a stretch of the Brenner–Bolzano railway line, summer 1943. *NA*

A vehicle of SS-Nachr.-Abt.1 of the Leibstandarte while crossing the Alps, August 1943. *NA*

The SS-Panzergrenadier Division Leibstandarte SS Adolf Hitler was among the first German units to reach Italy, within the context of Plan Alaric (the invasion of Italy) and Plan Achse (the disarmament of Italian troops). Initial plans called for the entire II.SS-Panzer-Korps to be transferred to the Italian front, but the difficult situation on the Eastern Front ultimately limited the transfer of only the Leibstandarte. On August 1, 1943, the first elements of the division reached Innsbruck, where the division was to assemble prior to its transfer to Italy, traveling through the Brenner Pass. The SS units formed march groups that reached Italy during the first week of August, moving to occupy the area of Po plain. On August 6, the division's commander, SS-Oberführer Theodor Wisch, set up his headquarters in Verona before moving it to Garda two days later. On August 7, the crews of II./SS-Pz.Rgt. LAH received their new PzKpfw.IV tanks at the stations in Parma and Reggio. They were joined three days later by I./SS-Pz.Rgt. LAH, which had been reequipped with PzKpfw.V Ausf.D Panther tanks. In the meantime, the Leibstandarte units that were already located in the area between Verona, Bolzano, and Trento were employed in reconnaissance missions to obtain information on Italian troops deployed in the Po plain, to determine their communications centers, and to check bridges to ascertain their load capacity. It was also necessary to determine if the border-crossing points were occupied or not.

Between August 9 and 12, the various units issued their reports: they had noticed many movements and arrivals of Italian troops in the Brenner sector and at the Reschen Pass.

A PzKpfw.IV of the Leibstandarte in the Parma area. *NA*

Leibstandarte vehicles on a road in northern Italy, passing a group of young Italians, possibly former Regio Esercito soldiers who have been demobilized. *NA*

Italian soldiers captured by the Germans, September 1943

SS-Obf. Teddy Wisch then issued an order indicating the line of conduct the division should assume in case of Italian defection: despite unambiguous agreements between the OKW and the Italian Comando Supremo (High Command) for the protection of the alpine passes in the Brenner area, which was supposed to be a joint mission between German and Italian troops, the Italians attempted to push the Germans from the fortified area, sending in alpine troops (which at that time amounted to two divisions), and to take control of or block all of the main roads in the South Tyrol. On the evening of August 17, the Leibstandarte was ordered by II.SS-Pz.Korps to assemble around Parma, Reggio, and Borgoforte (Mantova). The areas garrisoned by Italian troops had to be identified so that they could be seized by quick raids and disarm the occupants. In order to accomplish this mission, scattered across the Po plain, in addition to II. SS-Pz.Korps, Heeeresgruppe B had available the LXXXIV.AK (76.Inf.Div., 94.Inf.Div., and 305.Inf.Div.) and LI.Geb.AK (44. Inf.Div., 71.Inf.Div., Brigade Dölla). The Italian troops were much more numerous but divided as to how to behave with respect to the Germans. On August 19, SS-Pz.Gren.Rgt.2 LAH took up positions in the Reggio–San Polo d'Enza–Scandiano area. The SS units continued to engage in reconnaissance missions for the next few days.

On September 3, the chief of staff of II.SS-Pz.Korps, SS-Oberführer Werner Ostendorff, forwarded the dispositions for the disarmament and internment of Italian troops. The measures were to be taken after receipt of the code word *Nordwind*. The Leibstandarte had the mission of keeping ready a strong combat group that was to maintain control of the roads between Verona and the Brenner Pass. On September 7, Teddy Wisch went to Innsbruck to deal with the divisional logistics units that were still located there.

Disarming the Italian Troops

On September 8, SS-Ostubaf. Georg Stolz (Div.1b), coming from Parma, reported that the civilian population displayed its joy over the peace concluded between the Allies and Italy. Leaflets began to circulate that read, "*Pace, pace, pace*" ("Peace, peace, peace"). The Leibstandarte headquarters staff then tried to contact II.SS-

Leibstandarte troops in the process of disarming Italian troops in Parma. *NA*

Italian officers surrendering. *NA*

Turin, September 1943: SS-Stubaf. Schiller of the Leibstandarte, speaking with Italian officers through an interpreter. *NA*

Pz.Korps by phone, but all of the lines had been cut. A message sent by radio also went unanswered. In the absence of Teddy Wisch, who was in Innsbruck, SS-Stubaf. Rudolf Lehmann (Div.1a) gave the following order to all units: "The news of the armistice between the Italians and the Anglo-Americans has been spread. Take measures to begin to march within the hour. Avoid any incidents." It was not until 2025 that II.SS-Pz.Korps was able to break radio silence: "Highest state of alert. J Day 9.9.1943 at 0100." The code name *Nordwind* was quickly transmitted to all units. At 2300, the corps made it known that an Italian air force noncommissioned officer (NCO) had warned the Germans that Anglo-American troops were getting ready to land at the airport in Reggio. As a precautionary measure, the Leibstandarte armored regiment was sent there. On September 9 at 0100, in conformance with orders, units of the Leibstandarte took up positions in front of the gates of Italian garrisons to disarm them. Assignments were as follows: I./2 and the SS-Stug.Abt. in Verona, I.SS/Pz.Rgt. and III./2 in Reggio, the SS-Pi.Btl. in Mantova, the SS-Aufkl.Abt. in Fornovo, and the SS-Wi.Btl. in Castellucchio (Mantova). Operations were carried out throughout the morning with the III./2 at Scandiano, the Stab 2.SS-Pz.Gren.Rgt. at Albina, the III./SS-Art.Rgt. at S. Polo, and the II./SS-Pz.Rgt. at Cadeo (Piacenza). The only resistance encountered by units of the LAH was at Parma, at the local officer school. Attacked at 0200 by the I./1, reinforced by I./SS-Art.Rgt., the Italians did not lay down their arms until 0930.

On September 10, the division continued with its mission to disarm the Italian garrisons in the region south of Lake Garda, Brescia, Bergamo, Novara, Torino, Cuneo, Mondovì, Asti, and Alessandria, and the Po valley as far as Cremona. SS-Pz.Gr. Rgt.2[1] was the first unit to set off on the march toward Turin. At around 1115, elements of its supply column were taken under fire at Pavia. This resistance was cut short by the Div.Sicherungs. Kp., commanded by SS-Hstuf. Karl Richter, and by Verst.19. Kp./2, commanded by SS-Ostuf. Rudolf Schlott. During these actions, the SS units suffered one killed and one wounded. At 1130, SS-Pz.Gren.Rgt.1, reinforced,[2] approached Milan from three different directions. Fortified positions were reported on both sides of the Treviglio road. SS-Ostubaf. Frey then had a parley with the commander of the Italian forces, General Vittorio Ruggero. In the meantime, around noon, the forward elements

A checkpoint manned by an Italian soldier and a soldier of the Leibstandarte Adolf Hitler in the Milan area, September 1943. *NA*

Sforzesco Castle, Milan, September 1943: Italian and Leibstandarte soldiers on guard duty. *NA*

Rifles confiscated from Italian soldiers. *NA*

of SS-Pz.Gren.Rgt.2 reached Settimo, a suburb of Turin, where the inhabitants reported that armed communists were causing disorder in the city. At 1430, SS-Ostubaf. Hugo Kraas reported that the commander of the Italian forces in Turin had ordered his troops to lay down their arms. At 1500, II./SS-Pz.Korps announced via radio that several Italian units in southern Italy were fighting against the Germans and that the Italian fleet had fired against elements of the Kriegsmarine. As a consequence, Italian officers and soldiers were to be treated as prisoners of war; at the same time, it was necessary to deal with individual volunteers and units that had been organized, up to battalion level, who instead had chosen to remain alongside the Germans, equipping them with weapons taken from Italian depots. At 1510, II./SS-Pz.Korps ordered the garrison at Vicenza to be disarmed. SS-Stug.Abt. LAH, commanded by SS-Stubaf. Von Westernhagen, dealt with that mission, after having been engaged in Verona.

SS-Aufkl.Abt. LAH, reinforced by 1., 10., and 11./SS-Art.Rgt. LAH, was employed at Brescia and Bergamo. SS-Stubaf. Knittel had to negotiate with the commanders of the two garrisons. In Milan, it became known that General Ruggero had ordered his troops to disarm the armed Communist groups inside the city. In return, he asked for the right for his soldiers to remain armed, and a guarantee to allow his soldiers to leave the city with honor of arms. During the evening, SS-Pz.Gren.Rgt.1 continued its approach march toward Milan, reaching the city's suburbs. Continuing to be subordinate to it was I./SS-Pz.Rgt. LAH. Meanwhile, in Turin the situation continued to become critical. Rudolf Sandig's II./2 managed to occupy the main roads into the city. Nevertheless, during a firefight near the railway station, one soldier was killed and one was wounded. On September 11 at 0303, Hugo Kraas reported that the Communist demonstrators had been disarmed by Italian soldiers. Shortly thereafter, his regiment rolled into the city as planned.

At Milan, following talks between Frey and Ruggero, it was agreed that the SS units could enter the city but that Italian soldiers would remain armed. In no case could any armed soldier leave the city. A quarter of an hour later, Leibstandarte troops went into Milan, reaching the center of the city at 0755. In other cities (Brescia, Riva, Cremona, Vercelli, Novara, Alba), disarmament proceeded without incident. In Turin, as well, all went well except for a firefight near the Fiat works. The following transfer of Italian prisoners by train toward Germany, however, led to serious difficulties, especially with respect to their feeding. In addition, fearing Allied bombing, many civilians left Turin. The absolute ban against leaving the city could not thus be enforced, due to the lack of available forces. At 1258, SS-Ostubaf. Frey telephoned Lehmann; the occupation of Milan was proceeding as planned, but there were not enough troops to occupy all the key locations, in particular the railway station, the main post office, the airport, and the army supply depots. At 1300, Lehman thus asked II./SS-Pz.Korps to make available all the units that were then at Verona and Mantova. At 1650, the first convoys of prisoners were put on the march from Pavia, Turin, Brescia, Cremona, and Parma toward Mantova, where the SS-Wi.Btl. LAH was charged with taking care of them. At 1700, SS-Aufkl. Abt. LAH reported that upon its entry into Bergamo, three hundred occupants of the prison had been released; forty were quickly apprehended. At 1745, almost all the units reported that the departure of the convoys had been prevented by the civilian populace. At 1810, a general appeal was made in Turin. On September 12, the disarmament of the garrison in Milan was completed without incident, as recounted by Heinrich Burk of the 7.Kp./SS-Pz.Rgt.1:[3] "We began to march toward Milan after noontime on September 12, in the midst of a great heat. In the evening we reached the suburbs. There the cannons were pointed and aimed as a demonstrative act. The civilians who thronged around the panzers had been informed that we were to attack the next day. The 3rd Platoon was to occupy the stations of Porta Romana and Porta Vittoria and defend them. Whenever the platoon commander [*Editor's note*: Ernst Inmann] was not around or when he was in good humor, we would carouse around the city and go to check the area around Porta Vittoria. It was really a 'strange war.' We spent at least two or three weeks like that."

On September 13 at 0650, Hitler ordered the division to place an officer at the disposal of Signora Mussolini in Forlì. SS-Hstuf. Gerd Steinert of SS-Pi.Btl. LAH was assigned this mission. During the morning, the reconnaissance group and the antitank battalion began to march to go to the assistance of SS-Pz.Gren.Rgt.1 LAH in Milan. In Turin, disarmament of the garrison was completed by 0900. The civilian populace was troublesome, but order was soon restored by the threat of reprisals. A general strike

An Sd.Kfz.250/1 of 13.Kp./2 on the march in the Mantova area. *NA*

Leibstandarte armor in the streets of Milan. *NA*

The crew of a Leibstandarte PzKpfw.IV in Milan. *NA*

was ended during the course of that same day. At 1130, 11.Kp./2 reported that the barracks at Cuneo had been evacuated by Italian soldiers and that it had been looted by civilians. Around noontime, 18.(Aufkl.)Kp./2, under SS-Ostuf. Rudolf Dix, which had been sent toward the French border, returned without having run into any Italian troops. At 2210, SS-Pz.Gren.Rgt.1 LAH reported that it had to prevent local civilians from looting a military installation in the Lambrate neighborhood. The division then ordered that unit to occupy the installation as well as all the other arms and ammunition depots in the area. The balance of operations by Leibstandarte between September 11 and 13 was truly impressive: 68,036 Italian soldiers had been captured, as well as an enormous amount of different types of arms and equipment, including ten artillery pieces, forty-nine antiaircraft guns, twenty-seven tanks, forty-six antitank guns, 270 mortars, 428 machine guns, 38,591 rifles, and 391 aircraft!

On September 14, operations continued with the disarming of lesser garrisons, such as those at Varese and Como. Reconnaissance parties were sent toward the Susa area, near the French border. Beginning on September 12, the I./2 had been engaged in occupying the area situated between the Swiss border and Novara. Between September 15 and 16, occupation of localities close to the border continued. The division's reconnaissance group cleared the Aosta region without meeting any resistance, while III.(gep.)/2 was engaged in the Cuneo area.

Italian Volunteers in the Leibstandarte Adolf Hitler

Between two and three hundred Italian soldiers were integrated into the Leibstandarte immediately after September 8. Among these, as mentioned previously, was Ferdinando Gandini, assigned to a company of SS-Pz.Gren.Rgt.1 LAH. His testimony reads as follows:[4] "It was September 15, 1943, I remember the day well. I was walking along Corso Buenos Aires, the major street where my house was located in Milan. I was thinking about what was torturing me, and I kept on going over what was on my mind and bothered my soul. I felt confused, uncertain, incapable of any decision. I had almost reached the end of Corso Buenos Aires, a few houses away from my own, near the great square of Porta Venezia and its public gardens. On the left, in Viale Piave, was the Hotel Diana, where the Germans had set up their headquarters. At that moment, near the headquarters, I saw a small German truck coming up the street. Next to the driver was a corporal, or maybe an NCO, who impressed me because of his imposing height, his calm gaze, and his nonchalant and simple demeanor. I felt his gaze upon me; it seemed that those eyes were looking at me firmly but with severity as well, as if saying, 'You're also a soldier, and until yesterday you were fighting alongside me, you were a comrade; have you now become my enemy?' I didn't really know what to do and what to think. In that instant the truck stopped and I approached it almost automatically. I was very undecided, and inside me was

Ferdinando Gandini wearing the Waffen-SS uniform. *Gandini*

conflicted. Reasoning with me and myself, I told myself, 'What's this story about the war against the Anglo-Americans being over if they are continuing to invade Italian soil and are bombing our cities every day? If there is an enemy, you need to continue to fight; you can't not continue to fight and abandon an ally like this!' My sense of honor felt wounded; I knew that it was easier to hide in a cellar or in the mountains and wait for events to play out, but as far as I was concerned, the sense of honor and the concept of homeland that had been drilled into me since I was a child called me like an imperious order that I could not, that I was unable, and that I did not want to ignore. A strong feeling of pride still dominated my thoughts and my soul. Among combatants, a strong sense of camaraderie develops. The comrade becomes a brother with whom you can get angry, to the point that you can fight, insult each other, or rob his shoes or cigarettes or the dog-eared photo of a naked woman (not in the German army, where theft was punished by shooting!); in other words, anything can happen as a result of the difficulties caused by living together in an anomalous and distressing situation, but . . . at any moment of shared life, the comrade is more than a brother—you defend him to the death in every circumstance, you help him, you give him aid, you love him, you cry if he is killed! You run to face any risk for your comrade, you carry him to shelter or to safety if he is wounded by enemy fire, and for him you would die. There, this feeling of camaraderie made me feel guilty facing that soldier who was looking at me with that clear, calm, and almost magnetic gaze. Two blue eyes of an angel, innocent, sincere, which fixed upon me, accused me: 'You were my comrade and you abandoned me!' I continued to mull this over and to repeat to myself: 'But what's this story that the Americans, who until yesterday were the invaders, have now become our liberators? If we're still fighting, it means that there is an enemy and that the values of honor and country force us to continue to fight. You can't go back on your word! My, our ally is the German soldier, and it is with him that I want to continue to fight!' I didn't make any political judgments or any subtle analysis; my mind reasoned according to my instinct, my feelings, and at that moment I acted and reasoned by impulse.

"I had not forgotten life at the front, the freezing cold, the hunger, the filth, the lice, the nervous tension, the constant danger, the nightmare of ambushes, the fear, the desperate cries of the wounded, the blank stares of dead comrades. Certainly, I could have continued to hide at home seeking to escape danger and taking advantage of the uncertainty of the times. My year group had not yet been called for obligatory draft duty; I could lie about ever having been a soldier, but I would never have been able to convince myself, ignore everything, and not listen to my own sentiments, which at that moment pushed me urgently and called to my sense of duty. The German soldier looked at me with a smile; perhaps he had understood by my expression that I wanted to transmit my thought, that I wanted to say, 'No, I did not betray you; I was caught up by things greater than me, events outside of and above and beyond my own wishes!' I approached him and tried to talk to him even though I didn't know a single word of his language. On the other hand, he did not understand a word of Italian but tried to listen to me with patience and courtesy. I felt an immediate and spontaneous sympathy for this soldier, who was perfect in his uniform, proud, simple, and kind in the way he listened to me; he had understood that I wanted to communicate something important to him. I felt that with the attempt to switch sides, we had committed a rotten trick, an undignified and vile act, and every Italian, knowing the vindictive nature of the Germans, was afraid of reprisals. We were guilty of an act of betrayal that never before had happened in the history of the world, by any civil nation worthy of the name. I explained that I was an Italian soldier, a Blackshirt, but the German didn't understand any of what I was saying. He said, '*Ein Moment!*,' made me get on the truck, and ordered the driver to get going. I was not afraid but instead had a sense of protection, of brotherhood, of warmth, almost of affection. I was brought to the Hotel Diana, where the Germans had their headquarters. When we got there, the NCO asked for an interpreter, who acted as a go-between between me and Otto Lundius, as the German soldier was called. So I told him I was a Blackshirt, a volunteer in the 'M Battalions' and, showing him the red 'M's that I had saved, wrapped in a handkerchief in my pocket, explained that those were my unit insignia. I added that I wanted to continue to fight alongside them and also said other things that I can't remember. I should have never said it: the soldier hugged me, then told everyone present who I was, and then I don't know what else in German, which for me was incomprehensible. Abandoning the typical rigidity of German soldiers, everyone seemed happy to see me as the comrade who had not betrayed them, a soldier who had retained his feelings of honor and loyalty intact. Understanding that the surrender of Italy had surprised and confused not only me as well as other Italians, but above all the Germans, who, as allies, saw themselves treated as enemies and hated as though there had not been three years when we fought hard side by side. The Germans could not understand the ease by which, from one moment to the next, the Italians had changed front and flag! That was foreign to their mentality, their education, their pride. Most of the Italian populace saw the Germans as the main cause of their misadventures and their troubles; they blamed them for the grave fault of having deluded them with their stunning victories, which now were a thing of the past, while the reality of the moment was the bitter defeats that had brought the war to our shores. All of a sudden, a large part of the Italian people had begun to consider the German allies as enemies, while the Anglo-Americans who had invaded Sicily and were working their way up the peninsula had become liberators and allies. . . . Ten minutes later I was in a German uniform, armed and equipped splendidly, and a soldier brought me by truck to say goodbye to my mother, because the German unit to which I was attached was ready to leave. . . . The company to which I was assigned was billeted near the Duomo of Milan and was equipped with tanks and armored cars. It was part of the SS Leibstandarte Adolf Hitler division, a Waffen-SS formation, special and elite units of the German military. . . . I didn't even know the division I was attached to, I knew nothing of it except that I had heard vague mention of the SS Leibstandarte Adolf Hitler, the most prestigious division in the German military, the combat unit that had never suffered a defeat, and facing which no enemy unit had ever been able to stand up against. I was enlisted in this division, although I did not come to know about it until later."

SS-Uscha. Gandini on the Eastern Front

SS-Gruppenführer Wolff giving an award to an Italian volunteer in the Italian SS Legion, November 1944. *Corbatti*

Chapter III
THE ITALIAN SS LEGION

Two moments during the liberation of Mussolini by German paratroopers and Otto Skorzeny, September 1943

Hitler greeting Mussolini after his liberation. *DW*

Soon after his liberation from prison on the Gran Sasso on September 12, 1943, Benito Mussolini expressly asked Hitler to form two Milizia divisions under Waffen-SS command, to be employed against Allied forces on the Italian front. They were to consist mainly of men coming from Milizia units and from army units that had distinguished themselves at the front during earlier campaigns. The Italian volunteers were to wear the SS uniform but would have Italian collar tabs with the lictor's fasces. On the basis of Mussolini's request, beginning as early as in mid-September, Reichsführer-SS Heinrich Himmler ordered that all Italian military personnel who wished to continue to fight alongside Germany, both from the army and the Milizia, were to be gathered together in a single camp.

On September 24, 1943, Himmler officially announced the birth of the Italian SS Legion (Italienische Waffenverbände der SS) as *Bestandteil* (affiliated) with the Waffen-SS. Its main function was to be that of supervising the formation and training of new Italian military formations, following the model of other foreign volunteer legions. On October 2, 1943, Himmler again issued a special order[1] for the formation of Milizia units, in which the requests of Il Duce were partially fulfilled. It was however decided to first form battalions to be employed immediately in the fight against partisan bands in northern Italy. After having gained some experience and having eliminated the rebel threat, these battalions were to have again been transferred to training camps to form the first regiments, and later, after their employment on the Italian front, the first Italian division would be formed in order to fight on the front line against Allied forces. A second division was to be formed the following year. Himmler also ordered that the Milizia volunteers would continue to wear the Italian uniform, but with SS collar tabs and insignia, using tabs with a red background instead of the normal black. These early Italian personnel were designated as the Waffen Miliz (Armed Militia), the fighting unit of the Italian SS Legion.

SS-Brigadveführer Peter Hansen

Italian soldiers drawn up for inspection at Münsingen. *Corbatti*

SS-Standartenführer Gustav Lombard

Personnel of the 97th Battalion. *Brunetti*

The Münsingen training camp in Württemburg, 25 miles (40 km) south of Stuttgart, was chosen for the headquarters of the volunteer group At the same time, a massive propaganda campaign was launched to spur the recruitment of the greatest possible number of volunteers. It should be borne in mind that during that same period, there were discussions underway for the creation of a new army for the Repubblica Sociale Italiana [*Translator's note*: the RSI (Italian Social Republic) was the puppet government headed by Mussolini]. On October 9, 1943, there were already 13,362 men at the Münsingen camp, soon to reach some 15,000. As with all German units being formed, an *SS-Ausbildungsstab* (formation and training unit) was created, commanded by SS-Brigadeführer Peter Hansen.[2]

Unable to assume command because of convalescence, SS-Standartenführer Gustav Lombard,[3] coming from the SS Florian Geyer cavalry division, took temporary command of the Italian unit. At his side, designated as chief of staff, was SS-Obersturmbannführer Johann Eugen Corrodi von Elfenau,[4] one of the first Swiss volunteers in the Waffen-SS, also coming from Florian Geyer. An Italian liaison detachment (*Verbindungsstab*) was also established, consisting of Italian officers under the command of Lieutenant Colonel Vittorio De Paolis, with the mission of assisting and coordinating the work of the *SS-Ausbildungsstab*. In addition to incorporating the Italian volunteers already at Münsingen, the combat element of the Italian SS Legion was fleshed out with other volunteer groups coming from Prague, Debica, and from Greece. The groups of Italians did not, however, remain at the camp at Münsingen but were repatriated shortly after completion of their training cycle.

The Miliz Regiment De Maria

Among the first Italian units to be completely integrated into the Waffen Miliz was the Miliz Regiment De Maria, commanded by Milizia consul Paolo De Maria (a Milizia consul was the equivalent of a colonel).[5] Prior to September 8, the consul was in Spalato (now Split), commanding the 89th Blackshirt Legion Etrusca; the unit consisted of about 1,500 men structured with the 89th Blackshirt Battalion of Volterra, the 97th Blackshirt Battalion of Siena, and a machine gun company. The 9th Battalion was commanded by the *primo seniore* (first senior, equivalent to a major) of the Milizia, Carlo Federigo degli Oddi, the future commandant of the Italian Waffen-SS units on the Anzio-Nettuno front. During the day of September 8, the personnel of the legion were in the Drnis area,

Soldiers of the XCVII Battalion in a 1942 photo. Among them is Consul Paolo De Maria, third from the left in the first row. *Giachetti*

General Karl Eglseer, commander of the 114.Jäger-Division

Blackshirts of the LXXXIX Etrusco Battalion of Volterra. *Brunetti*

along the Dalmatian coast, attached tactically to the Bergamo infantry division. On September 9, 1943, the Bergamo headquarters issued orders to fall back to Sebenico (now Sibenik) and to resist any attacks by the Germans. Units of the SS Prinz Eugen division and the 114.Jäger-Division were located in that area. After he had discussed the situation with his men, the entire legion passed over to the German side. That same day, De Maria met with General der Gebirgstruppe Karl Eglseer, commander of the 114.Jäger-Division, to discuss the terms of transfer of his unit into the German armed forces.

De Maria requested and was granted assurances that his unit would not be used against other Italian units, and was promised that his men would be armed and equipped adequately in order to be able to continue to fight against their previous enemies. The German commander accepted those terms, and thus the legion was officially subordinated to the 114.Jäger-Division. Following the example of the militia personnel, other groups of soldiers from the Bergamo and other Italian units present in the area made the same choice, voluntarily choosing to fight alongside the Germans. In all, roughly three thousand were thus integrated into a Polizei-Freiwilligen-Verbände (volunteer police troops) of the German Ordnungspolizei, commanded by Oberst De Maria. The men continued to wear their old uniforms, with a white armband on the left arm of the jacket with the word *Ordnungspolizei* on it. Along with German units, the unit was soon employed as a security force against partisan formations.

On September 27, the Miliz Regiment De Maria was ordered to leave the Drnis area and to move toward Knin, still in the hands of Italian units. The entire garrison there joined the regiment. From Knin, the march resumed aboard trucks toward Bihac, and from Bihac by train to Belgrade. From the Serb capital, still by train, following a series of mistaken movement orders, the Italians ended up first in Austria and then in Berlin, which they reached on October 5. Because of the great confusion of the moment, and above all because of the anti-Italian climate that was rampant in German circles following the Badoglio about-face, the members of the regiment were placed in a prison camp. There was great delusion among the men, and when on October 12 they were asked if they still wanted to continue to fight alongside the Germans, many refused the offer; in fact, there were more than a thousand defections. On October 15, the Miliz Regiment De Maria, with two thousand men remaining, was transferred to Münsingen, where it arrived two days later. Because of overcrowding in the camp, De Maria's personnel were "set up" in the nearby camp at Gensewak. When in November 1943 the battalion returned to Italy, it was officially designated as the 1o Reggimento Milizia Armata (1st Armed Militia Regiment), with headquarters in Milan, still commanded by Waffen-Standartenführer De Maria. The I Battalion was commanded by Waffen-Obersturmbannführer Federigo degli Oddi, the II Battalion by Waffen-Sturmbannführer Vittorio Gori, and the III Battalion by Waffen-Obersturmbannführer Giorleo.

Two photos of Oberst De Maria at Münsingen. *On the left*, speaking with other Italian officers in the camp; *on the right*, while he inspects a guard picket consisting of Italian soldiers. *Corbatti*

Two high-ranking officers of the Armed Militia at Münsingen. *Corbatti*

Scharführer Walter Morini, one of the first volunteers in the Debica. *Morini*

The Fedelissimo Battalion

Another Milizia unit that chose to join the Waffen Miliz in its entirety was the XIX Battalion Fedelissimo, which was stationed in the Balkans and consisted mainly of volunteers who were from Lombardy. In early September 1943, the battalion was stationed in the Preveza area along the Ionian coast of Greece, subordinate to the Acqui infantry division. Its commander, Milizia first senior Gilberto Fabris, upon notice of the armistice, gathered his men to express his desire to continue to fight alongside the Germans. The battalion followed him unanimously. The 1.Gebirgs-Division, under General Stettner, was in the area, which was quickly contacted by Fabris to discuss the fate of his unit. The battalion, duly transformed as the Bataillon Fabris, was subordinated to the 98.Gebirgsjäger-Regiment and employed along the coast as a security force against partisan bands, as well as in defense of the coast. The unit remained subordinate to the German mountain division until the beginning of November, when it began its transfer to Italy in the Waffen Miliz, which was not completed until December 1. Stationed in Aosta, the unit became the XI Battalion of the Waffen Miliz.

SS-Bataillon Debica

At the Debica training camp near Krakow, in what was then the General Government, the most battle-tested battalion of the Waffen Miliz was formed, which would be designated with the name of that Polish locality. The story of this unit began in October 1943 at the camp at Feldstetten, some 12 miles (20 km) northeast of Münsingen. There a group of interned Italian prisoners accepted the proposal of Major Guido Fortunato (former commander of the XIX Battalion of the 6th Bersaglieri with the CSIR [Corpo di Spedizione Italiano in Russia; i.e., the Italian expeditionary corps in Russia]) to constitute a special Italian SS unit. Fortunato, one of the first Italian officers to stand alongside the Germans, had been authorized to circulate among the various prison camps to seek new volunteers. Of the four hundred soldiers who answered his call, only thirty-eight were declared unfit, with the remainder transferred to Münsingen for initial training. In early December, Fortunato and his cadre of volunteers from Feldstetten, reinforced by several hundred other volunteers (twenty officers and 571 men), were transferred to the SS-Truppen-Übungsplatz Heidelager, east of Debica.

This was a special school for the German SS where divisional reconnaissance units were trained, and through which may foreign personnel had also passed. The training of the volunteers was much more difficult and intense than the training had been at Münsingen, which transformed the Italian volunteers into proper Waffen-SS combatants. For that reason, the unit was designated from the outset as the SS-Bataillon Debica (its official designation was the Italienische SS-Freiwilligen Bataillon), while all the other units of the Waffen Miliz were unable to wear the SS insignia. The volunteers wore German uniforms and wore the black SS insignia.

Waffen-Stubaf. Fortunato

Soldiers training at the SS-Truppen-Übungsplatz Heidelager. *Leol*

Italian Armed Militia volunteers coming from the alpine troops. Note the metal death's-head badge affixed to the cap to attest to belonging to the Waffen-SS. *Corbatti*

The Units Are Fleshed Out

The Italian volunteers in Münsingen were organized into twelve battalions. The first three battalions formed the 1o Reggimento Milizia Armata (1st Armed Militia Regiment), born from the transformation of the Miliz Regiment De Maria. Because of the number of officers available, an officers' battalion was also formed. Men deemed unsuited for combat were formed into a labor battalion, to be used in building defensive works rather than on the front line. Members of the *carabinieri* corps were organized into a camp security unit. With respect to weapons and equipment, the Italian volunteers continued to wear their old uniforms. The German command distributed the metal "death's head" insignia to all the volunteers, to be applied to their jacket lapel or to their headgear, constituting the only official identifying symbol for members of the Waffen Miliz.

On November 11, 1943, the Italian volunteers took the oath of allegiance to Adolf Hitler:

Before God I make this sacred oath:
that in the struggle for my Italian homeland
against its enemies I will be absolutely
obedient to Adolf Hitler
supreme commander of the German army
and as a valorous soldier will be ready at all times
to give my life for this oath

Once the ceremony was finished, the volunteers were told of their imminent return to Italy. At the same time, they were offered the chance to be transferred into the forces of the Italian Social Republic or into other Waffen-SS formations. About a thousand volunteers chose to join the ranks of the RSI, while only about a hundred elected to join other Waffen-SS units. There were also a number of defections; about five hundred volunteers preferred to return to prison camps after a false notice had been circulated about a possible transfer of Italian SS units to the Eastern Front. Prior to returning to Italy, specialized personnel of the Waffen Miliz, about a hundred men, were sent to various specialty schools at Dachau, Weimar, Dresden, and Stettin.

Volunteers of the Armed Militia, coming from the ranks of the Italian Royal Navy. Note also in this case the metal death's-head insignia on the berets. *Corbatti*

Return to Italy

On November 17, 1943, the official order was given for the Waffen Miliz to return to Italy. The Waffen Miliz, an auxiliary formation of the Waffen-SS, was directly subordinate to the commander of the SS and police in Italy, SS-Obergruppenführer Karl Wolff. There were thirteen Waffen Miliz battalions coming from Münsingen and Prague, and once they were in Italy, they were deployed to the Po plain area, far from the front and with internal security duties, to deal with the growing threat posed by partisan bands. The following table shows the location, commanders, and strength of each battalion:

Battalion	Location	Commander	Officers	NCOs	Troops
1st	Milan	Milizia major Carlo Federigo degli Oddi	25	99	568
2nd	Milan	Major Vittorio Gori	28	100	573
3rd	Milan	LTC Armando Giorleo	25	100	573
4th	Turin	Major Erono Giona, replaced by Major Del Soldato	27	56	617
5th	Bologna	Major Giorgio Marzoli	31	47	624
6th	Cuneo	Captain Tullio Traverso	30	101	576
7th	Casale	Major Michele Michelini	28	85	576
8th	Como (Lecco)	Major Carlo Pace	25	100	573
9th	Lucca	Milizia major Francesco Tognetti	30	99	574
10th	Trieste	Milizia major Valentino Fracasso	29	96	384
11th	Aosta	Milizia major Gilberto Fabris	31	72	371
Officers	Ferrara	Colonel Luigi De Pietri Tonelli	634	24	136

SS-Obergruppenführer Karl Wolff

Cremona, SS volunteers looking at posters at Boccasile. *Corbatti*

A thirteenth battalion, consisting of volunteers deemed not fit for combat, upon arriving in Italy was put at the disposition of the German police as a "work detachment." The three battalions (1st, 2nd, and 3rd) stationed in Milan with a regimental headquarters company (thirty-four officers, thirty-four NCOs, and 339 soldiers) formed the 1st Regiment of the Armed Militia (Waffen Miliz) commanded by Milizia consul Paolo De Maria. In addition to these 8,585 volunteers (976 officers, 1,103 NCOs, and 6,596 other ranks), there was also an Italian staff of the Italian Waffen Miliz, located at Vago (Verona Province) under Lieutenant Colonel De Paolis, consisting of thirteen officers, forty-five NCOs, and 136 other ranks. The 6th Battalion, stationed in Cuneo, was the first of the battalions to be employed against the partisans. On December 9, it was attached to a German unit and sent in to attack the partisans at Boves who had dug in at Vinadio, in Valle Stura. After a day and a half of tough fighting, the Italian and German SS force overcame the resistance of the partisans, who were dispersed. The Italian SS battalion reported the loss of two men, plus one severely wounded.

Early Employment of the Debica

The Debica Battalion was sent to Pinerolo in late February 1944, following three months of training billeted in a former alpine troops barracks. On March 12, the men received new uniforms originally intended for German paratroopers. The battalion was still subordinate to Waffen-Sturmbannführer Fortunato, and the three companies that it consisted of were under the orders of Waffen-Hauptsturmführer Cantarella, Dal Dosso, and Premuda. The unit was soon engaged in actions against the partisans.

On March 21, 1944, the Debica was sent to Val Pellice, south of Turin, to take part in antipartisan Operation Spärber, along with a battalion of the 15th SS Police Regiment and several RSI units. During the operation, which ended on April 1, the partisan forces in the valley were scattered but not wiped out. The Debica was engaged in very hard fighting in the city of Rora, where the commander of the

Debica troops on the march during an antipartisan operation. *AC*

SS-Oberführer Erich Tschimpke inspecting Italian volunteers. *AC*

Generalmajor der SS Piero Mannelli, the legion's inspector of enlistment as of March 1944, with the SS volunteers at Rodengo-Saiano. *AC*

SS-Ostubaf. Konstantin Heldmann

2nd Company, Dal Dosso, was seriously wounded. In addition to him, the battalion suffered the loss of one other and five seriously wounded. For high valor demonstrated during the action, volunteer Giovanni Fois was awarded the Iron Cross Second Class, while Waffen-Hauptsturmführer Dal Dosso was awarded the Wound Badge in Silver for having been wounded in combat. Following Operation Spärber, the Debica remained in Val Pellice until April 12, 1944.

The Italian Assault Brigade

In January 1944, drawing some personnel from the Waffen Miliz headquarters, a general staff of the Italian volunteer legions was formed under von Elfenau, who had been promoted for the occasion to the rank of *SS-Standartenführer*; this new military echelon was to deal mainly with organizing a new combat unit drawing on the best personnel of the Armed Militia and recruiting new volunteers. Also within the Italian SS Legion, a heavy-weapons inspectorate was formed, which was to see to the training and formation of artillery units. Consisting of German personnel, it was placed under the command of SS-Obersturmbannführer Konstantin Heldmann.[6] An artillery group commanded by Major Carlo Pace and an antitank group commanded by Major Pietro Mannelli were subordinated to the heavy-weapons inspectorate. On February 9, 1944, the 1a Brigata d'assalto (1.Sturmbriagade der italienische Freiwilligen Legionen, or 1st Assault Brigade of the Italian Volunteer Legion) was formed, commanded by SS-Brigadeführer Hansen. It was not yet a true Waffen-SS unit; in fact, the Italian volunteers still used the Wehrmacht rank insignia and wore tabs with a red rather than black background. The uniform worn by the volunteers was a mix of Italian and German items. Equipment was generally scarce and varied, the leftover fruits of German and Italian depots. The jacket was Italian, the pants of various types, including those of the paratroopers (*rundbundhosen*) or those of the Italian army. Some volunteers wore the German belt with the center buckle; ranks and insignia were German, in red (they became black only for those volunteers who fought on the front line). Helmets were the Italian army type, with the SS insignia painted on in white. As for other foreign volunteers, an armband was created with a lictor's fasces on it, made in Germany, but this was never actually distributed to the Italian volunteers. Also made in Germany was a special insignia with the lictor's fasces on a black background, but it too was never distributed.[7] The distinctive symbol of the Italian SS became an eagle made of metal, with the lictor's fasces worn on the left arm of the uniform rather than the usual National Socialist eagle, or of the version in cloth, but was also worn on field caps. This insignia was expressly requested by Il Duce to symbolize the Fascist origin of the volunteers. The Italian Assault Brigade was organized with two regiments (1. and 2.Infanterie-Regiment), each of three battalions: the 1st Regiment (I, II, and III Battalions) was commanded by Colonel Peghini, and the 2nd Regiment was commanded by Colonel Enzo Celebrano. On March 6, 1944, Himmler established that "the Italians who had sworn allegiance to the führer and fought in the SS or in the Wehrmacht could receive all the same awards as German soldiers." Beginning in March 1944, throughout the territory of the Italian Social Republic, recruitment centers were activated for the Italian SS run by the Inspectorate for Italian Legion volunteers, answerable to Waffen-Generalmajor der SS Piero Mannelli and SS-Oberführer Erich Tschimpke,[9] assisted by twenty-nine principal and six secondary officers. The walls of Italian cities were covered with posters that urged young men to join the Waffen-SS for the honor of the country and to continue the fight alongside their German comrades. Enlistment notices also appeared in the newspapers.

A German soldier at the Anzio bridge head, smiling at war photographer Grönert for a propaganda photo. *NA*

Chapter IV
THE NETTUNIA FRONT

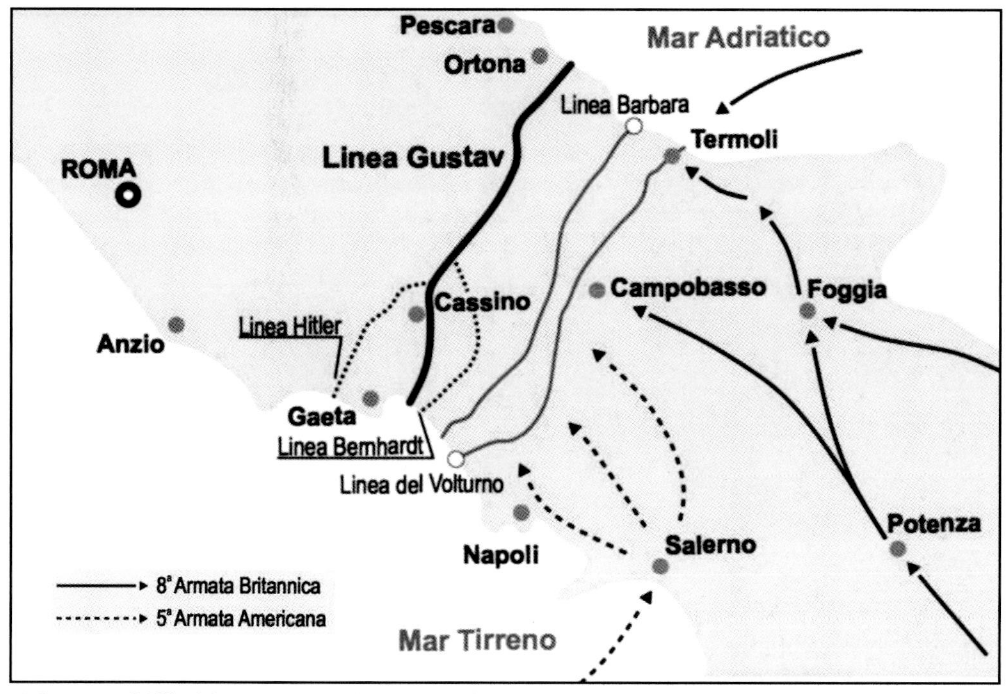

Advance of Allied forces toward Rome and German defensive lines

Feldmarschall Albert Kesselring

Troops and amphibious craft landing on the Lazio coast, 1944

In January 1944, during the long advance up the Italian peninsula, the American forces of the 5th Army had reached the German Gustav defensive line, which ran along the Garigliano River. Encountering stiff resistance, especially in the Cassino sector and along the Rapido River, the Allied headquarters planned to strike the rear of the German forces, landing an expeditionary corps on the shore between Anzio and Nettuno; at that time, the two communities had been unified as a single municipality called Nettunia. The VI Corps, under General Lucas, was to have landed behind the German lines at the same time, since there was to be a frontal attack launched against the Cassino sector. In this way, the VI Corps would have cut the German lines of communication between Rome and Cassino and isolated the German 10th Army.

The first landings took place on January 22, 1944 (Operation Shingle), and by the next day fifty thousand Allied soldiers were on dry land: Allied VI Corps consisted of the British 1st Division and the US 45th Infantry Division, plus numerous US Ranger and British commando units. The Germans had very few forces in the sector. Shortly following the Allied landings, it was possible to send only a few flak and artillery units and some armored vehicles to the area. But the Germans improvised quickly to send all the available forces they could, taking advantage of the fact that Lucas, the American general, instead of quickly pushing inland, wanted to wait for the landing of heavy artillery and tanks.

That same day of January 22, at the bridgehead, Feldmarschall Kesselring shifted troops of the 4.Fallschirmjäger-Division, stationed in Perugia, and the Fallschirm-Panzer-Division Hermann Göring, stationed in the Priverno area in the province of Latina, to the bridgehead. The 16.SS-Panzergrenadier-Division Reichsführer SS was still being organized and, with its men

SS-Gruf. Max Simon, commander of 16.SS-Panzergrenadier Division Reichsführer-SS, with other officers in Ljubljana, January 1944

SS-Stubaf. August Dieterichs. *Dieterichs*

SS-Ostubaf. Fritz Knöchlein

A German Panther at the bridgehead

scattered between Italy and Slovenia,[1] was also alerted. On the morning of that same day of January 22, the order reached the headquarters of the SS division to form two combat groups to transfer to subordination of the new 14.Armee, commanded by General Mackensen (I.Fallschirmkorps and LXXVI Panzer-Korps), which faced the bridgehead. The first *Kampfgruppe* was formed with elements of II./SS-Pz.Gr.Rgt.35, commanded by SS-Sturmbannführer August Dieterichs,[2] consisting of veterans of the Sturmbrigade, while the second was formed with personnel of II./SS-Pz.Gr.Rgt.36, stationed at Ljubljana and initially commanded by SS-Sturmbannführer Fritz Knöchlein,[3] and then from mid-March by SS-Hstuf. Herbert Vetter.[4] The march of the two *Kampfgruppen* to the combat area was quite confused, especially that of Kampfgruppe Knöchlein, both because of the lack of enough transport and the bad weather conditions and Allied aviation.

The leading elements of Kamfgruppe Dieterichs, billeted at Lucca, arrived in the area as early as January 24. The two *Kampfgruppen* did not complete their moves until the end of January and were deployed along the Mussolini Canal (now the High Water Canal) between Borgo Podgora and Borgo Flora, subordinate to 715.Infanterie-Division. Reichsführer-SS troops did not take part in the German counteroffensive that began on February 16 (Operation Fischfang), which attempted to annihilate the enemy forces that had landed, and developed in the area between Cisterna and Fosso della Moletta, in the northern part of the bridgehead. They were instead engaged in limited attacks against American forces (the 504th Paratroop Regiment) deployed along the Mussolini Canal, particularly the SS grenadiers of Kampfgruppe Knöchlein. Even though they were supported by several army assault guns, the SS companies suffered heavy losses, but nevertheless their action prevented the American paratroopers from sending reinforcements to the sector between Cisterna and Aprilia. On February 28, another attack was carried out by a company of Kampfgruppe Dieterichs toward the crossroads south of Borgo Flora, while another company of Kampfgruppe Knöchlein was to seize the bridge over the Mussolini Canal north of Borgo Podgora. Neither objective was taken, mainly because of the small size of the forces engaged in the actions.

On the left: Mussolini speaking with German officers. *On the right*: the German military commander in Rome, General Kurt Maeltzler, reviews troops of the Barbarigo prior to their transfer to the Anzio front.

Milan, Adriatica barracks, March 1944. *From the left*: Ustuf. Pio Filippani-Ronconi, Ostubaf. Carlo Federigo degli Oddi, and Leutnant der Schutzpolizei Karl Häsecker, liaison officer in 1. Kompanie.

Arrival of Italian Units

Shortly after the Allied landings between Anzio and Nettuno, Benito Mussolini expressly requested that Kesselring immediately send Italian SS units to the bridgehead. Kesselring replied a few days later, informing Il Duce that SS-Ogruf. Wolff had already authorized the immediate outfitting and arming of the Italian SS troops and their movement to the front line, along with paratrooper personnel of the Nembo who had also joined the German side. In fact, as early as February 12 the first contingent of Italian paratroopers reached the bridgehead. On March 3, it was the turn of the Barbarigo naval infantry battalion of the X Divisione MAS to be deployed in the southern part of the front.

Its 1st Company fought alongside men of Kampfgruppe Knöchlein. Aware that employment of the Italian SS units was being delayed, Il Duce again requested their immediate dispatch to the combat zone. Thus, around mid-February, SS-Ogruf. Wolff ordered the headquarters of the Italian SS legions to quickly form a new battalion of the 1.Sturmbrigade to be employed on the southern front against the Allies. Therefore, SS-Standartenführer Karl Diebitsch[5] was charged with forming a *Kampfgruppe* consisting of the three battalions of Infanterie-Regiment 1 of 1.Sturmbrigade; the best personnel were concentrated in the II Battalion, led by Ostubaf. Carlo Federigo degli Oddi, structured with three companies and a headquarters company. In the end, this was the only unit that was able to be prepared for the front, subordinate to Kampfgruppe Diebitsch, along with a support unit and a field hospital. The III Battalion served to provide replacements for the "Degli Oddi," while the I.SS-Bataillon Debica was engaged in antipartisan operations until the end of May 1944. On the eve of its departure from Milan, the battalion consisted of thirty-two officers, ninety-three NCOs, and 525 men. The volunteers were armed with 421 91/38 carbines, 131 Beretta MAB submachine guns, 130 Beretta pistols, fifty Breda model 30 light machine guns, twelve Breda model 37 heavy machine guns, and ten 81 mm mortars. There was also a German liaison element with the unit consisting of Schutzpolizei officers and several interpreters. The unit left Milan by train on March 13 and did not arrive south of Rome until a week later, during the night of March 19–20. The area of the front was

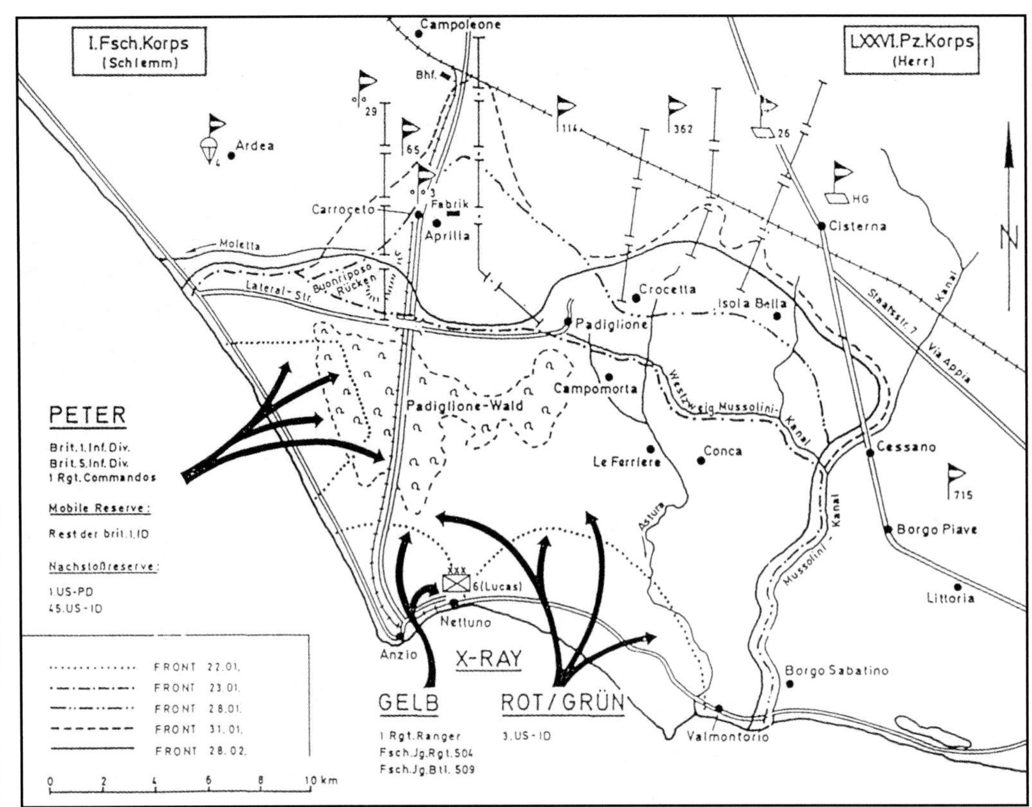

Map of the bridgehead with the front line trace between January and February 1944

A German soldier with an MG42

A Kampfgruppe Dieterichs defensive position on the Anzio front. Note the shallow foxhole because of the swampy terrain prevalent in the area.

German soldiers in the Anzio bridgehead

reached by truck, where Kampfgruppe Diebitsch was assigned to LXXXVI Panzer-Korps and attached tactically to 715. Infanterie-Division. The Italian SS troops took up positions between two combat groups of the Reichsführer-SS; the first to go into the line were the grenadiers of 1.Kompanie under Hstuf. Buldrini, in the II./SS-Pz.Gr.Rgt. 35 sector. The next day, 2. and 3. Kompanie were assigned to the II./SS-Pz.Gr.Rgt.36 sector.

Several platoons of 2.Kompanie relieved the 1st company of the Barbarigo in positions along the Mussolini Canal, veterans of terrible fighting in which they had taken heavy casualties. The choice of the sector assigned to the Italian SS troops was not by chance; the German headquarters selected a relatively quiet sector of the front to better integrate the Italian volunteers into the German defense scheme, and, to that end, were positioned alongside SS troops of the *Reichsführer*, who were considered most reliable. Of the Italian companies, only 3.Kompanie, led by Hstuf. Comini, was given its own sector of the front, inserted between the positions of 5. and 7.Kompanie of II./SS-Pz.Gr.Rgt. 36 (Kampfgruppe Knöchlein). The two other companies were split into platoons that were assigned to various companies of the *Reichsführer-SS*; in particular, those of 1.Kompanie among the companies of Kampfgruppe Dieterichs and those of 2. Kompanie among those of Kampfgruppe Knöchlein.

The headquarters of the Italian SS battalion and the support detachment assumed positions near Sermoneta, while the field hospital was set up at Abbadia. The defensive line along which the Italian volunteers were engaged ran along the Mussolini Canal and the Fosso di Cisterna; this line was protected by barbed wire and minefields, with many forward positions defensed by legionnaires. The first real obstacle to deal with was the nature of the terrain, which was damp and wet, which made it impossible to dig holes deep enough to provide cover from enemy fire. The Germans greeted the Italians quite reluctantly, and it was only the test of fire that made them change their minds. The Italian legionnaires fought without ever being

German defensive positions on the Anzio front, March 1944: they are similar to First World War trenches.

Ustuf. Filippani-Ronconi. *Filippani-Ronconi*

German soldiers under enemy fire, May 1944

relieved, in an unnerving war of position in wet foxholes, engaged mainly in reconnaissance missions and raids behind enemy lines. In addition to those who fell in combat, rheumatic illness and malaria also took their toll.

To better coordinate actions against enemy positions, an Arditi platoon was formed, consisting of some thirty men of the 1.Kompanie, commanded by Ustuf. Filippani-Ronconi and Ustuf. Nicandro Bovenzi. During a night action at Borgo Flora on April 14, Ustuf. Filippani-Ronconi was seriously wounded by a mine. His place was taken by Uscha. Cavicchi, who was killed in combat at the end of May. Filippani-Ronconi was the first volunteer from the battalion to be awarded the Iron Cross Second Class; six other Italian legionnaires received the same award shortly thereafter. On the pages of issue 4 of *Avanguardia*, the Italian SS newspaper, the first article on the employment of the Italian SS appeared: "On thc Nettuno front, during the course of patrol actions and enemy infiltration attempts, units of the Italian SS Legion decisively counterattacked and quickly reestablished the prior situation. The volunteers of the new Italy, tested by fire, demonstrated excellent combat spirit, and great morale."

On April 15, troops of the *Reichsführer-SS* were pulled from the front line. They were replaced by troops from 715. Infanterie-Division. The Italian SS troops remained in their same positions. During the night of April 28–29, the Arditi platoon was engaged in retaking a strongpoint near Borgo Flora. The Americans were thrown from the position, leaving seven prisoners in Italo-German hands. An enemy counterattack made about an hour later by an American company supported by armored vehicles and artillery fire was quickly repulsed. Ustuf. Bovenzi was wounded in the action. To face off against the enemy tanks, the Italian volunteers were instructed in the use of the *Panzerfaust*, while the brigade headquarters received six 75 mm Pak 40 antitank guns with their crews. To make up for the heavy losses sustained during the fighting (after a month, about 150 men were out of combat, among whom were thirty killed), Ostubaf. Degli Oddi was forced to accept about fifty volunteers who arrived directly at the front, almost all of whom were very young. Reinforcements later arrived from the brigade, mainly from III./R.1.

Photos of Waffen-SS soldiers taken by SS-Kriegsberichter Hermann Grönert on the Anzio front in spring of 1944. In the first two photos, *left and center*, these are almost certainly Italian volunteers, considering the facial features and the fact that they are still wearing parts of the Fascist militia uniform, the first wearing an overcoat and the second wearing a Mod. 40 jacket. Note that both volunteers are wearing black collar tabs with double runes. The photo on the right is of a soldier of the 16.SS-Panzergrenadier Division Reichsführer-SS. *NA*

AVANGUARDIA

LA LEGIONE IN COMBATTIMENTO

DAL FRONTE DI NETTUNO

La croce di ferro a cinque legionari

Fra questi vi è un ragazzo di 17 anni che tutte le notti va di pattuglia

In poche settimane di fronte i volontari della Legione SS Italiana si sono talmente distinti che cinque nostri camerati sono stati decorati sul campo della Croce di Ferro di II Classe. Aderendo ad una nostra richiesta, il Col. Brigadiere Diebitsch ci ha inviato una corrispondenza sulle sue impressioni nel corso della cerimonia per il conferimento delle Croci di Ferro e su quelle nel corso di una visita ai nostri feriti. Nella lettera indirizzata alla nostra direzione egli scrive che i volontari italiani stanno bene e ancor meglio combattono, anche se negli ultimi giorni la battaglia è diventata più aspra. I camerati germanici sono molto fieri della decisione e dello spirito combattivo dei nostri Legionari.

ZONA DI OPERAZIONI, X.

Sono passate più di quattro settimane da quando i primi volontari della giovane Legione SS Italiana hanno raggiunto la linea del fuoco a fianco dei camerati della SS Germanica, per dare il loro contributo, per cancellare l'onta gettata su di loro dal tradimento del re e di Badoglio e per riconquistare la libertà alla Patria.

Sono state settimane dure, notti gelide, pioggia e fango. Oggi splende il sole e attorno la primavera è già in fiore. E' dome-

lato, biscotti, bustine di zucchero, tè, ecc.).

Un'altra volta, è sempre in scena il maresciallo C., in servizio di pattuglia con 7 uomini di cui 3 pionieri della Wehrmacht che conoscevano bene l'ubicazione delle zone minate, si era incontrato con una pattuglia nemica.

IL MIO BAMBINO

E' nato un bimbo: il mio bambino è nato e la notizia dell'avvenimento,

KURT KURBERZIG

(Trad.: Serg. A. Nicolini)

In un ospedale militare

Un solo desiderio: tornare a combattere

Zona di operazioni, aprile.

DAL FRONTE DI NETTUNO

In prima linea tra il fango le bombe e il buon umore

A venti metri dal nemico – Di notte i legionari si sgranchiscono le gambe con audaci azioni di pattuglia – Fuochi d'artificio notturni, mentre la Luftwaffe e l'artiglieria pesante bombardano i porti nemici

From issue 6 of *Avanguardia*, April 22, 1944

The Iron Cross

(From issue 7 of *Avanguardia*, dated April 29, 1944)

In only a few weeks on the front line, the volunteers of the Italian SS Legion have so distinguished themselves that five of them were awarded the Iron Cross Second Class in the field. Colonel Brigadier Diebitsch sent us correspondence regarding the ceremony for the award of the Iron Cross, as well as his visit to our wounded. In the letter addressed to our editors, he writes that the Italian volunteers are well and fight even better, even though in the last few days the battle has become bitter. Our German comrades are very proud of the decisiveness and combat spirit of our legionnaires.

Operational Zone

More than four weeks have passed since the first volunteers of the young Italian SS Legion have reached the front line alongside their comrades from the German SS, to make their contribution, to cancel the shame put upon them by the betrayal of the King and Badoglio, and to regain the liberty for the homeland. They have been hard weeks, with freezing nights, rain, and mud. Today the sun is shining and springtime is flowering around us. It is Sunday, a day like any other at the front, and everyone is aware of it. All is quiet at the front; not even a shot can be heard, and only a few aviators are making curves in the infinite blue background of the sky.

On the left, five Italian SS volunteers awarded the Iron Cross Second Class by SS-Obf. Diebitsch in early May. *From the left*, Ustuf. Massimo Flick, Uscha. Oceanico Fiaschi, Uscha. Giovanni Grandi, Uscha. Pietro Orlandoni, and the seventeen-year-old legionnaire Ermenegildo Mascitti. *De Palma*

In the photo on the right, an Italian SS Legion poster hung on a wall in Padova

Ermenegildo Mascitti, awarded both classes of the Iron Cross. *Saronno*

The metallic outlines of the planes shine in the sun. We are next to an old house, behind which rise the Alban hills, hills with their cultivated terraces and groves of olive trees, dotted with small mountain towns that are so characteristically necessary for this landscape. A unit of Germans and Italians, wearing helmets and combat gear, are drawn up on parade. The allies stand across from each other, and between them a small group of five Italian volunteers from the Italian SS legion are just as they have come from their trenches. They are the legionnaires who distinguished themselves by particular courage and who now are being awarded with the Iron Cross for their actions. The commander of a German regiment in whose sector the Italian legionnaires were engaged has just arrived with his officers. Quick, sharp commands, the German and Italian honor guards present arms, the battalion commander presents the force, and we pass in review. The commander, with military brevity, speaks to underline the solemnity of the moment. It is the first time that the Iron Cross, this magnificent military order, is bestowed upon volunteers of the Italian SS Legion. Faithful to their oath, these men fought. Enemy fire made them tougher and stronger, and in action they gained the esteem and recognition of their German comrades. The red, white, and black ribbon of the most beautiful military award shines with its vivid colors, and the black cross with its silver border sparkles in the rays of the sun. But the eyes of the soldiers upon whose chests the decoration is hung sparkle just as well. They are five men for whom this day of honor on the Nettuno front will remain unforgettable: a young second lieutenant—who by quick initiative and decision threw an enemy assault group from its position; two NCOs with strong, lean faces who distinguished themselves in several patrol actions; a boy of seventeen years, a Balilla, who from the first day, almost every night, went out on patrol and gathered important information; and, finally, another young legionnaire, wounded and just released from hospital. He trembles with emotion when the Iron Cross is hung on his chest, and his eyes sparkle with joy. A "Sieg heil!" (Victory!) addressed to the führer, the supreme commander of the German armed forces, concludes the brief ceremony.

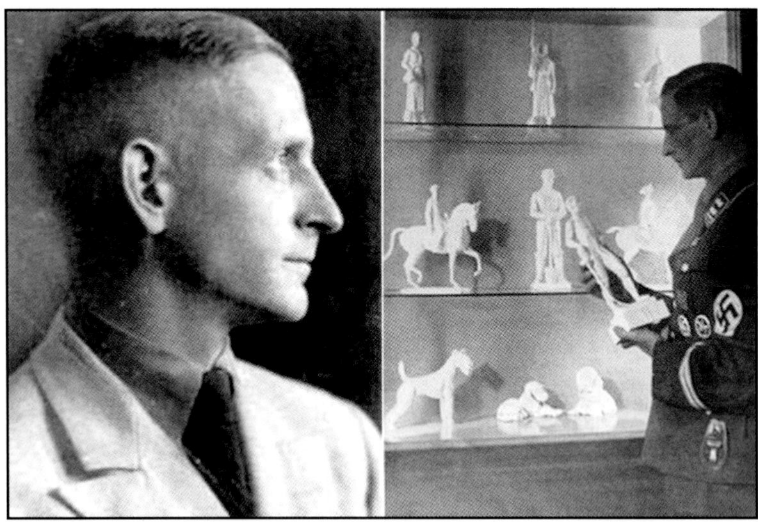

Two photos of Karl Diebitsch, in civilian clothes and in uniform

German soldiers on the Anzio front. *NA*

DAL FRONTE DI NETTUNO

GIOVANI EROI DELL'ITALIA REPUBBLICANA

La bella morte del legionario Ferrero - L'audace impresa del S.ten SS Flick - Un indimenticabile ordine del giorno - Ora si parla del sergente Coco - Le più belle pagine sono ancora da scrivere

Corrispondenza di guerra del Serg. SS A. Niccolini

Gli episodi di valore si susseguono ininterrottamente e non passa giorno senza che venga segnalato almeno un fatto degno di essere ricordato. Giovani e veterani si contendono in una nobile gara la palma della gloria e dell'eroismo e sarebbe difficile precisare se siano i « Vecchi » (così sono chiamati, dai « Balilla » i veterani) con l'esempio delle loro gesta passate e presenti ad insegnare ai giovanissimi il segreto della virtù militare, o siano i neofiti, i « Balilla » a ridestare in essi, col loro slancio e col loro entusiasmo, le speranze e gli ardori che li fecero cavalieri dell'onore e del-situato sull'argine del Canale Mussolini a soli 30 metri dalle postazioni nemiche, hanno tenuto a bada, dopo aver dato l'allarme e suscitato il fuoco incrociato delle nostre armi automatiche, una pattuglia americana forte di 40 uomini. Feriti, l'uno a una spalla da una scheggia di granata, l'altro ad un braccio, continuano a sparare arrestando il movimento del gruppo nemico fino a che il S. ten. Flick (testè decorato di croce di ferro di seconda classe) si slancia di sua iniziativa, con quattro uomini, in aiuto al posto attaccato e con un nutrito lancio di bombe costringe risate che si espande liberamente in barba agli anglo-americani, i quali, dalle postazioni vicinissime, certo si domanderanno come si possa ridere così di gusto alle 5 del mattino dopo una notte insonne trascorsa sotto un martellamento di granate. Ma il silenzio ritorna ben presto: del sergente Coco si sa sempre ben poco; ogni tanto combina una prodezza e questa volta si è guadagnato addirittura la citazione sull'ordine del giorno da parte di un ufficiale come l'Oberfuhrer Diebitsch: val proprio la pena di ascoltare.

Il serg. Z narra l'ultimissima: comandante di posto avanzato, assalito dal nemico trattiene la foga dei suoi uomini e lo lascia avvicinare fino a 10 metri circa. Allora lo accoglie con una scarica di bombe a mano che lo mettono in fuga facendogli lasciare nelle nostre mani un mitragliatore, due pistole automatiche e un prigioniero. « Questo è il serg. Coco, e di questa tempra è il I Battaglione della Brigata « Vendetta ». Ma le più belle pagine le dobbiamo ancora scrivere ». Le parole del sergente Z suonano alle orecchie di tutti come un monito e una promessa.

L'EROICA MÒRTE DEL SERG. MAGG. SS GIOVANNI FERRERO

Ordine del giorno N. 65

1) Il Comandante Supremo della SS ha disposto, per ordine del Führer, la costituzione della I Brigata Italiana Granatieri SS.

2) In base a questo la I Brigata d'Assalto della Legione SS Italiana porterà, con effetto dal 27-4-44, la suddetta denominazione.

Ciò significa un riconoscimento del Comandante Supremo della SS per l'attività svolta da ufficiali, sottufficiali e legionari.

F.to WOLFF

SS Obergruppenfuehrer u. General der Waffen SS - Capo Supremo della SS e della Polizia in Italia - Comandante della Legione SS Italiana

Comunicazione

Il Comandante Supremo della SS e della Polizia in Italia e Comandante della Legione SS Italiana ha disposto che venga concesso il diritto di portare le mostrine nere della SS alle unità della Legione SS Italiana dopo la loro prova al fronte.

Con la prova data in modo completo è previsto per queste unità, come ulteriore riconoscimento, un distintivo particolare — simile a quelli portati da valorose Divisioni germaniche — sulla mostrina destra che, per il momento, rimane sprovvista di ogni contrassegno.

Il Comandante Supremo della SS, Reichsfuehrer Heinrich Himmler, su proposta del Generale Wolff, ha già concesso alle unità della Legione SS Italiana impegnate sul fronte di Nettuno l'autorizzazione di fregiarsi delle mostrine nere.

From issue 10 of the newspaper *Avanguardia*, dated May 20, 1944, testimony of war and official communiques

LA LEGIONE IN COMBATTIMENTO

Il legionario Esposito uscì di pattuglia e rientrò con sette americani

Con cinque proiettili in corpo il volontario Gennaro aggrappandosi a sterpi di grano si trascina sulla terra e sfugge così alla cattura

Corrispondenza di guerra del Serg. SS A. Niccolini

Da qualche minuto le granate dei mortai nemici picchiano sul canale di Cisterna. Le rane che gracidavano felici ai primi ... to a due pattuglie, una di camerati della Wehrmacht forte di 10 uomini coadiuvati da 5 guastatori, l'altra composta di 10 no- ... possa emettere un sol grido. Intanto, per il varco aperto, gli altri arditi entrano nella postazione e vi sorprendono due ameri-

Un padre ci scrive

Tutto per la Patria

Ponderano, 9-5-1944-XXII

Cara « Avanguardia »,

Ho ricevuto ieri il primo numero in abbonamento e nel secondo elenco dei Caduti della SS Italiana figura il nome del mio carissimo figliuolo Vincenzo.

Nella desolazione in cui siamo piombati ci è di conforto la sicurezza che è morto per la nuova Italia, per la sua Fede.

Ecco un periodo della lettera inviatami da lui in data 23 novembre da Milano:

« Carissimi tutti,

« Finalmente dopo due mesi ritorno in Patria; provengo dalla Germania ove ho avuto la gioia di incontrarmi col nostro caro Eugenio e di stare con lui un po' di tempo.

« Anche il caro Eugenio si è arruolato come me nella Milizia SS Italiana, con la vera unica idea di rimettere ordine e di rendere un po' d'onore alla nostra povera e bella Patria martoriata ».

Sicuro di interpretare il suo pensiero, e non potendo fare altro, ho versato L. 500 al locale Municipio « Pro armi alla Patria ».

Ti sarei grato se questa mia fierezza e la mia offerta fossero portate a conoscenza ai Volontari del 1° Battaglione SS Italiani, perchè ne traggano la certezza che i veri Italiani sono con loro e per loro, che non si battono invano, che vinceremo.

Sono vecchio fascista del '20 e repubblicano dal 1° ottobre 1943. Ho un altro figlio, Eugenio, puro lui nella

RICONOSCIMENTO D'ONORE

Il Comandante Supremo della SS, Reichsfuehrer Heinrich Himmler, quale riconoscimento per le dimostrazioni di valore e di senso del dovere dei volontari della Legione SS Italiana, ha diramato in data 3 maggio il seguente ordine:

« I reparti costituiti o da costituire in Italia, in quanto non si tratti di formazioni di polizia, sono considerati reparti della SS con tutti i doveri e con tutti i diritti ».

Il sangue e la vita dei nostri valorosi commilitoni schierati sul fronte di Nettuno, hanno guadagnato alla Legione questo altissimo riconoscimento. La parità di doveri e di diritti coi camerati della SS germanica costituisce il più alto onore e la più grande dimostrazione di fiducia che potevamo attenderci. Essa impegna tutti i comandanti e gli uomini al più alto rendimento.

RICOMPENSE AL VALORE

Un corriere dal fronte di Nettuno annuncia che, nel corso degli ultimi combattimenti, sono state conferite 12 Croci di Ferro ai nostri volontari. Il Maresciallo Graziani ha presenziato alla consegna di alcune di esse. Una cinquantina di legionari sono stati promossi per merito di guerra al grado superiore.

From issue 10 of the newspaper *Avanguardia*, dated May 20, 1944, testimony of war and official communiques

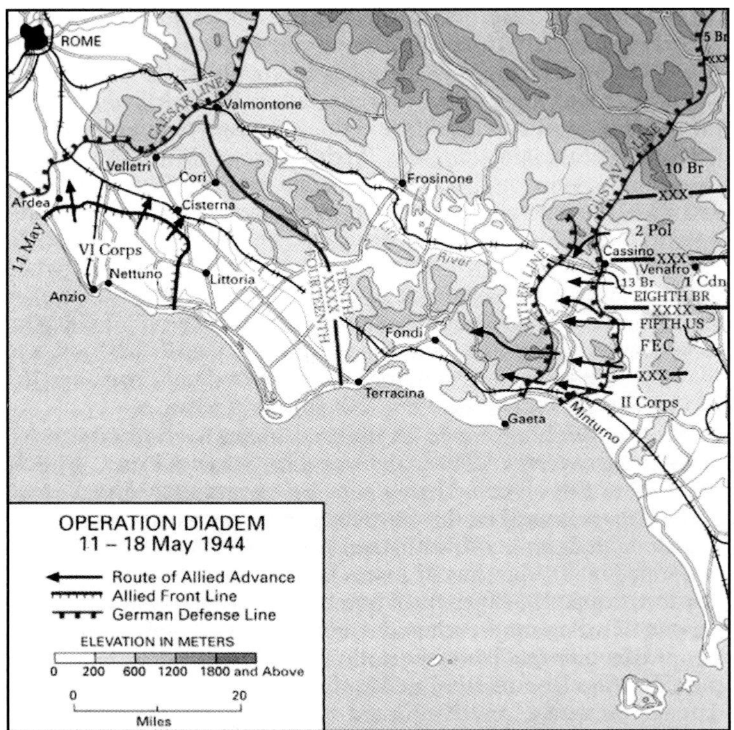

US Army Center of Military History, CMH Pub 72-20, p. 18

In this hour, once again the call is raised to the Italian people of all regions of Italy; once again the cry of faith is raised that must reach all active forces, because once again we have shown that the sons of Italy fight and wish to fight and do not want to remain behind and away from their German comrades. Here on the line are the legionnaires of the Italian SS, proud and happy. They lie in the field hospital peaceful and patient and anxiously await the day when they can return to the line alongside their comrades, for fresh battles and new victories. Once again: these men who wear the Iron Cross are not seeking recognition; they simply say, "We know that we have not done much; we only did our duty. But we will do better, because there is still much to do." And now they go back to the trenches, to their foxholes and little strongholds on the front line, they go back to their comrades, as examples, and I know that soon we will see others come here to receive, as these men have, recognition for their valor.

—SS-Oberführer Karl Diebitsch

The Allied Offensive

On May 2, 1944, the Allies launched a major offensive against Montecassino and the Gustav line (Operation Diadem), along with a contemporaneous attack by their forces against the bridgehead at Anzio, with the aim of surrounding and wiping out the German 10.Armee. With the fall of Cassino, after a week of horrific fighting, the American forces began a push against the German forces in the Cisterna area, beginning on May 23. The Italian SS defensive positions were particularly hard hit by the American attack; the Italian legionnaires, hunkered down in their foxholes and trenches, sought to hold out against the assaults by enemy infantry. Antitank defense was provided mainly by *Panzerfäuste*. The fighting was carried out in a climate of great confusion, with heavy losses on both sides. The American attack fell heavily upon the positions of 3.Kompanie, which was almost completely wiped out during the fighting. On the same evening of the twenty-third, the Americans had reached the Via Appia. The remnants of the Italian SS companies tried to regroup in an attempt to slow down the enemy advance as much as possible. What remained of 1.Kompanie was ordered to cover the withdrawal of the other units, taking up positions along the Via Appia and remaining there for the rest of the day of the twenty-fourth. SS-Oberführer Diebitsch and Ostubaf. Degli Oddi remained with the company and were the last to leave their

US soldiers prepare to cross the Mussolini Canal during the first phase of the offensive.

German half-tracks engaged in defensive combat during Operation Diadem, May 1944

positions. The men of 2.Kompanie were also engaged in covering the withdrawal of other German units before pulling back to the north, along with the support detachment.

SS-Oberführer Diebitsch managed to reach Tivoli. The other men ended up attaching themselves to various German units during the course of their withdrawal to the north. In Florence, a march headquarters was set up to collect all the surviving legionnaires and then to convoy them to Pinerolo; of the 950 legionnaires engaged on the southern front, only two hundred reached the Piedmontese city. The survivors were awarded twenty-two Iron Crosses Second Class and fifty-two field promotions from the Germans; Mussolini awarded ten Silver Medals plus the medal for the battalion's standard. In addition, by an order that was rendered official only on September 7, 1944, volunteers who had fought at the front were allowed to wear the black SS collar tabs in lieu of the red tabs. Finally, for all Italian SS volunteers, the rank terminology in use by the Waffen-SS was introduced. As of April 27, 1944, the Italian Assault Brigade officially became the Italian SS Grenadier Brigade (Waffen Grenadier Brigade der SS).

Young volunteer Bruno Fattori of Florence, awarded the Iron Cross Second Class and the Wound Badge in Gold and promoted in the field to the rank of *Unterscharführer. Corbatti*

The Debica on the Southern Front

On April 12, 1944, SS-Bataillon Debica, after having been motorized with thirty-two new Fiat 626 trucks and twelve motorcycles, was transferred to central Italy, to be attached to Kampfgruppe Diebitsch. The Debica was not sent to the Anzio front immediately but went to Spoleto to be employed in antipartisan actions along the Via Flaminia; the Germans were preparing to pull back to the north. Between April and May, Debica fought against partisan forces in the area around Nocera Umbra, Assisi, and San Severino Marche, losing fifty men among the killed, wounded, and missing. With the arrival of fresh volunteers, the strength of the battalion reached around five hundred men and twenty officers. On May 31, the battalion was moved to the Tyrrhenian coast to be employed in an antilanding role, south of Ladispoli and subordinate to 92.Infanterie-Division, which had just arrived from France. Following the rapid advance of Allied troops, on June 4, 1944, the order was given to withdraw to the north, toward Grosseto. The confusion of the moment led to the unit splitting up into various groups, which independently began to pull back to the north. The order,

American Sherman tanks destroyed on the Lazio front, May 1944

however, did not reach 1.Kompanie under Hstuf. Cantarella, which between June 5 and 6 found itself fighting against units of the US 36th Infantry Division near Palo Laziale, along with a battalion of 92.Infanterie-Division.

Particularly distinguishing himself in the fighting was the 1st Platoon, led by Oscha. Walter Morini, which several times risked being surrounded by the Americans. The survivors were finally able to attach themselves to a German battalion and also pull back to Grosseto. On June 16, the roughly two hundred remaining men of the Debica were collected in Florence for employment along the Gothic Line, which was under construction.

On the left: young SS volunteer of the Debica photographed during the battalion's retreat toward Florence in June 1944. *Corbatti*

On the right: An SS legionnaire from Debica armed with a Beretta MAB submachine gun on the street of a town in central Italy during the antipartisan operational cycle in spring 1944. *Corbatti*

Chapter V

EMPLOYMENT OF ITALIAN SS UNITS ON THE SOUTHERN FRONT

SS-Ostubaf. Johann Eugen Corrodi von Elfenau, chief of staff and then temporary commander of the Armed Militia from December 1943 to January 1944. *Corbatti*

La Legione SS Italiana

Attende i giovani che, oltre volere la Patria libera, grande ed onorata, sentano il dovere assoluto di essere solidali fino alla vittoria e, se occorre, fino alla morte coi valorosi alleati germanici.

UFFICI D'ARRUOLAMENTO
BRESCIA - CORSO ZANARDELLI, 36

Recruitment poster

German soldiers on the Anzio front

Staf. **Eugen Corrodi von Elfenau**
Report on the employment of the II Battalion of the 1st Infantry Regiment of the armed Italian units of the SS (March–May 1944) on the southern front (Nettuno)

I. Origins of the Battalion

At the end of November 1943, the volunteer formations of the Milizia Armata (Armed Militia)—now the Armed Italian Units of the SS—returned to Italy from the Münsingen training camp in Germany.

II. Constitution of the Battalion

In mid-February 1944, the Höchster SS. U. Polizei Führer in Italien ordered the preparation of a battalion of the former Milizia Armata drawn from personnel of the 1st Assault Brigade. This sudden employment originated mainly for political motives, because the German high command desired that units of Italian volunteers be employed at what was thought to be the ensured destruction of the bridgehead at Nettuno. In accordance with these orders, a march battalion was constituted within the 1st Armed Militia Regiment, stationed in Milan. The outfitting, equipment, clothing, and weapons were still lacking because of the limited availability, and training was likewise deficient. A host of significant problems had to be resolved. The personnel had been recruited from various specialties of the former Italian army: Blackshirts, infantrymen, alpine troops, bersaglieri, and drivers. Their equipment was thus a jumbled mixture. Overcoming these grave difficulties by hard work, on March 12, 1944, it was possible to ready a battalion.

III. Organization, force, and armament of the III Battalion, 1 Infantry Regiment

Structure: 1 headquarters company, 3 mixed companies
Strength: 32 officers, 93 NCOs, 525 other ranks; total 650
Armament: 424 Mod. 91 carbines, 131 Beretta submachine guns, 130 Beretta pistols, 50 Breda Mod. 30 light machine guns, 12 Breda Mod. 37 heavy machine guns, 10 81 mm mortars
Transport vehicles: None

IV. Transporting the battalion to the front, headquarters, and support

On February 21, 1944, the battalion's officers were received by Mussolini at his headquarters. The battalion left from Milan (Greco station) on March 13, 1944, at 0700. Arrival at Littoria station during the night of March 19–20. The II Battalion of the Infantry Regiment of the Italian Armed Units of the SS (known for propaganda purposes as I SS Bataillon Italia), commanded by Lieutenant Colonel Degli Oddi, was subordinate to Oberführer Diebitsch as commander of the *Kampfgruppe* because its other units were scheduled to be added later in order to constitute a combat group.

V. Employment (position warfare)

On March 21, 1944, the 1st Company entered the line near cisterna in the II./SS-Panzer Gren.Rgt.35 sector. On March 22, the 2nd and 3rd Companies went on the line between Cisterna-Mussolini Canal and Borgo Podgora in the II./SS-Panzer Gren.Rgt.36 sector. The 2nd Company relieved a company of marines of the Barbarigo Battalion, which after twenty-one days on the line, because of very heavy losses, was in urgent need of reconstitution. The men soon had to dig themselves in. The muddy ground presented great difficulties, because water was struck at a depth of only 60 centimeters (1.97 ft.). The positions for automatic weapons, mortars, rifle pits for infantrymen, and antitank positions had to be built completely from scratch, or the existing ones, which had been seriously damaged by medium and heavy (120 mm) mortar fire, had to be rebuilt.

German observation post on the Alban Hills, March 1944

A German soldier, March 1944

German soldiers cleaning their weapons in a defensive position on the Anzio front, in water and mud, 1944

A German patrol on the march at the Anzio front, March 1944

For the first few weeks, the men were heavily engaged in that hard work, carried out essentially at night, while during the daylight hours only the sentries were awake. In some positions, in order to achieve at least minimum shelter, the men were forced to keep their legs immersed in water and mud up to their calves. After a brief orientation of the ground that lay before them, intense patrol activity was begun, both to determine the enemy positions as well as to try to capture prisoners from enemy patrols or to carry out raids to wipe out or occupy enemy positions that were particularly troublesome or threatening to Italian lines. The battalion's activity, given the stabilization of the front, consisted almost wholly of such activity, but it is precisely that type of activity that wears down, tires, and reduces units with the steady stream of losses. The morale of the troops is, however, raised by daily small acts of valor. Patrols are normally made up of Italian and German personnel, varying in number depending on the task at hand. Command is assumed by an Italian or German officer of NCO who, in the opinion of the commander, is the "smartest of the bunch." Lately, there have also been many patrols consisting exclusively of Italian volunteers. Captured prisoners are shared among all units so that everyone can benefit from leaves that are granted for prisoners. Precious information regarding the enemy is thus furnished by our patrols to the headquarters of the two German battalions.

On April 18, the volunteers of the two German battalions are relieved, while the Italian legionnaires continue to remain on the line without relief until the end of the Nettuno bridgehead. Relations with the comrades from the two Wehrmacht battalions (I and II.Gren.-Rgt. Mot 1028) were very good and at times marked by cordial brotherhood, despite the difference in language and mentality. As a result of patrol activity and other engagements in late May, a total of about fifteen Anglo-American prisoners were taken, as well as large numbers of light and heavy machine guns, pistols, automatic rifles, and their ammunition. For important raids that required men of the utmost reliability and proven courage, some thirty men of the 1st Company, whose behavior was such that it earned a citation in the German corps' order of the day, were employed. Another case worthy of mention is the hand-to-hand counterattack by the mortar crews of the 1st Company, which allowed their comrades to pull back, but who, because of holding out along the line, would otherwise have surely been surrounded and overrun. That bold action was also mentioned in the German corps bulletin.

a. Awards for Valor

There were numerous acts of valor carried out by individuals, along with their German comrades, but it would take too long to list them here. These are reflected by awards for valor, by proposals made for awards for valor, and by promotions for acts of bravery. As of May 15, for acts of valor in the face of the enemy, the legionnaires of the battalion were awarded eleven Iron Crosses Second Class and fifty field promotions, and, for acts of valor in the face of the enemy (some in the presence of Marshal Graziani), around twenty proposals for awards for valor, some of which were posthumous, were forwarded to the Italian Minister of War, since they related to units that consisted entirely of Italians, except for three officers of the German SS who had liaison duties with the three companies.

La Legione al fuoco

I volontari della Legione SS Italiana sono già da parecchie settimane impegnati in vittoriose azioni contro l'invasore anglosassone e i sicari prezzolati delle « grandi democrazie » sul fronte di Nettuno e contro i nemici interni nelle valli alpine del piemontese. La stampa italiana ha dato notizia in questi ultimi giorni della seconda attività della nostra Legione, attività del tutto temporanea e dovuta in massima parte a ragioni di legittima difesa. « Avanguardia » ha invece già dato notizie della lotta contro lo straniero e continuerà a darle, perchè il motto della Legione è questo: « Fuori gli anglosassoni! ». Il silenzio molte volte è d'oro. I legionari della SS non si sono arruolati volontariamente per amore di elogi o di encomi, ma unicamente per servire con fedeltà ed onore la Patria italiana in una lotta che vede come unico premio meraviglioso la vittoria contro i nemici della unità, dell'indipendenza e della libertà dell'Italia.

Nel prossimo numero pubblicheremo delle corrispondenze sull'attività dei nostri arditi che, nel massimo silenzio e nella più assoluta disciplina, stanno dando la vita per l'onore del popolo italiano e per la rinascita della Patria.

Per ora vada a tutti coloro che colle armi in pugno affrontano quotidianamente la morte il nostro affettuoso pensiero. Sappiano che costantemente li accompagnano le benedizioni delle nostre donne e dei nostri bambini, sappiano che il patto d'amore verso la nostra Terra che essi suggellano col sangue e col sacrificio forma le basi della immancabile rinascita dell'Italia, potenza rispettata e direttrice nella solidale Europa di domani.

Viva la Legione!

From the weekly *Avanguardia*, issue 5, April 15, 1944

From the weekly *Avanguardia*, April 6–22, 1944 issue: Italian SS legionnaires attacking enemy positions

b. Losses
Following are the loss figures for the battalion as of May 20:

	Officers	NCOs	Troops
Dead	2	8	42
Wounded	7	27	135
Missing	1	7	58

Total losses 287 men

It should also be kept in mind those who were sick with malaria and rheumatic fever, which amounted to an average of fifty men who were missing from their units every day. This meant that the companies stayed on the line at much-reduced strength, and as a result, platoons with a strength of 15–20 men had to hold a stretch of the line more than 500 meters (1,640 ft.) long, engaging in "acrobatics" to prevent the enemy from infiltrating.

I nostri decorati

Dal fronte di Nettuno giunge la notizia che altri dieci volontari della Legione SS Italiana sono stati decorati sul campo della Croce di Ferro di II Classe. Vengono segnalate anche alcune promozioni per merito di guerra.

Un altro reparto SS in linea

Da alcuni giorni un nuovo reparto della Legione SS Italiana è giunto sul fronte di Nettuno. Alla prova del fuoco i nuovi arrivati si sono dimostrati degni dei commilitoni che li hanno preceduti.

Per i nostri feriti

Sulle rive del Lago Maggiore è stata scelta una magnifica residenza, dove passeranno la licenza di convalescenza i nostri valorosi feriti.

From *Avanguardia*, issue 9, May 13, 1944

German tanks and grenadiers at the bridgehead

Overall losses: until disengagement with the enemy: about 70 percent of the overall forces.

c. Replacements
The high losses of dead, sick, wounded, and missing and the men who were busy with indispensable services that increased daily continually reduced the battalion's strength on the line, thus making it necessary to assign replacements. This was not a simple problem, since almost all the brigade's units were engaged in combat against the rebels, and it had not yet been possible to provide all the equipment (especially transportation assets) needed to complete the units.

Initially the column led by Lieutenant Capelli was sent, consisting of three officers, three NCOs, and forty-one men who reached the battalion on May 3.

On April 27, the brigade had already readied a replacement company (Captain Fattovich) consisting of five officers, 240 NCOs, and troops, which left by train. Because of mistaken interpretation of orders, the unit was detoured along the way and employed in antipartisan activities in the Norcia-Spoleto area. As a consequence, the Fattovich replacement company was reduced to a strength of about 180 men and did not reach the front until May 21.

To remedy the mistake with the Fattovich company and its delay, another replacement unit was readied by the brigade (the Heimer replacement unit: one officer, twelve NCOs, and 121 men; total 134), which left for the front on May 15, 1944.

Because the battalion had also been assigned six 7.5 cm German antitank guns, in order to avoid drawing down even more men from the battalion, the brigade sent two officers, six NCOs, and thirty trained men.

Overall replacement totals: eleven officers, 393 NCOs, and troops.

VI. Anglo-American offensive and withdrawal

On May 20, 1944, around 1100, the enemy, without artillery preparation and using artificial fog, broke into the sector of the German platoon on the left flank of the 3rd Company II/1028 and took almost the entire German platoon prisoner. The enemy, in company strength, took up positions in a grain field behind the 3rd Company's line of resistance. A sweep took place during the night between May 20 and 21 and ended with the destruction or capture of the enemy. On May 21, the line of resistance was once again in the hands of the legionnaires. At that time, the enemy's intentions to begin the offensive were already clear. Artillery fire was relentless, and interdiction fire hit the access routes and the ground behind them almost without interruption. On May 22 at 0300, the enemy attack kicked off in grand style with heavy employment of tanks, following a two-hour drumbeat of artillery fire. There were significant losses along the main line of resistance, and the survivors were unable to hold their positions. Our men remained on the resistance line to the extreme limit of their possibilities, firing their last rounds against the American infantrymen who were following behind the tanks, holding off the tanks in close-quarters combat, hurling their last hand grenades against the tracks and vision slits of the tanks. On the night of May 23, the enemy reached the Via Appia. The scattered remnants of the battalion tried to regroup to form small pockets of resistance. The survivors of the 3rd Company, which had been exposed to the greatest enemy pressure and was almost wiped out, could no longer be employed. All is lost; there are no more reserve weapons. Officers and men are at the end of their tether after having been without rest for two months. Up until midnight on May 24, the 2nd Company held a strongpoint on the Via Appia at the crossroads with the canal, to enable a battalion of Luftwaffe troops on foot to withdraw from Littoria without running the risk of being surrounded. Behind our soldiers who marched toward the Cisterna-Cori containment line during the night of May 24–25, German motorized engineers blew bridges and roads. The battalion could no longer be employed along the successive containment lines because the battalion's food and ammunition columns along with those of the German 715.Inf.Div. (mot.) were destroyed and set ablaze on May 25, in the Giulianova plain during an attack by American fighter-bombers that lasted for more than seven hours. Following those events, the commander of the combat group of which the II.I.R.1 was part ordered the battalion to disengage from the enemy and called for the remnants of the battalion to regroup in the area to the rear of the zone of operations. The battalion had been on the line uninterruptedly for exactly nine weeks—from March 20, 1944, until May 25, 1944—distinguishing itself, in addition to exceptional feats of arms, for having managed to hold the vast section of the front amounting to almost 5 kilometers (3 mi.) while at the extreme limit of their capabilities. It served in an outstanding manner to replace German units that had been hard pressed during the bitter counteroffensive fighting in February in order to reduce the Nettuno bridgehead.

German soldiers captured in Cisterna, May 1944. *US Army Signal Corps*

The bridge over the Mussolini Canal along the Via Appia, where on May 24, 1944, the 2.Kompanie, led by Hstuf. Fiaschetti, was deployed to temporarily halt the advance of Allied units. *Corbatti*

A Sherman tank knocked out in the Cisterna sector, 1944

German defensive positions on the Anzio-Nettuno front with 88 mm flak guns, spring 1944

Something to eat right on the front line

VII. a. Support

To provide support to the troops, a headquarters was established that tended to the troops on the line, as well as to the wounded. Because of the energetic work of this support headquarters, during the withdrawal it was possible to remove the wounded to medical facilities in the rear area. Afterward, those wounded who were in need of a period of convalescence were sent to a rehabilitation center at Ghiffa (on Lake Maggiore), which in the meantime had been established for the Armed Units of the Italian SS.

b. Morale

For the first few weeks the morale of the men was excellent. As time wore on, it began to decrease, because bodies began to feel the effects of the not-indifferent sacrifices of prolonged life in the trenches. Other factors that significantly affected the troop morale were represented by

- not having seen, after more than two months on the line, the arrival of other Italian troops;
- the anti-German propaganda or deceit practiced by personnel who were, disgracefully, Italians coming from Norma, Cori, and Sermoneta and who circulated in the rear area; and
- the lukewarm enthusiasm that the great majority of families of the combatants showed in their letters (following letters that were intimidating or outright threatening by the rebels) and especially because of radio broadcasts made by British radio.

Despite all of this, in more than two months of tough fighting at the front against an enemy that had superior numbers and equipment, the II Battalion was able to shine the light fully on the characteristics of valor, courage, spirit of sacrifice, and the most absolute dedication of the Italian soldier of all times.

c. Official German assessments on the men of the II./1.R.1

The Wehrmacht battalion and company commanders with whom the companies of the II Battalion were employed expressed themselves as follows:

Captain Tornow, commander of II./1028 Grenadier Regiment: "The military bearing is rigid and disciplined. The behavior of officers, NCOs, and soldiers is very much desirous of combat and decisive. The unconditional will to fight is expressed by the five Iron Crosses Second Class that were awarded. The very high morale in combat has as its basis the fanatical intent generated by a pure idealism to reestablish the honor that was betrayed by their people. The brotherly collaboration between officers, NCOs, and Italian and German soldiers is quite good and sincerely felt by all parties."

LA ϟϟ ITALIANA IN AZIONE

Giudizi di ufficiali germanici

27 aprile 1944

« La collaborazione con i volontari italiani della SS è stata assai buona e non si ebbero assolutamente punti di attrito. La prontezza all'impiego di ufficiali, sottufficiali e uomini è stata sempre egualmente eccellente. Nelle azioni di pattuglia e nella difesa contro attacchi nemici essi si confermarono buoni. ...Il comportamento militare degli ufficiali è stato ineccepibile. Sottufficiali e truppa si sono adoperati con la più grande passione perchè venissero eseguite le disposizioni germaniche al riguardo. I camerati italiani in trincea sono sempre stati felici di combattere e di lavorare. Come giudizio sintetico io ho avuto l'impressione che gli uomini della SS Italiana sono gli idealisti del loro popolo, idealisti che hanno dolorosamente la coscienza del tradimento e tendono a ripristinare l'onore dell'Italia con l'impiego senza riserve della loro vita ».

Ten. Stuetz
Comte di un reparto sulla destra della SS Italiana

27 aprile 1944

« ... I sottufficiali dànno l'impressione di risolutezza e di spirito combattivo; la condotta militare è rigida e disciplinata. Nelle ispezioni ho sempre trovato le posizioni della SS Italiana pronte alla difesa ».

Ten. Juckenack

(Continua in terza pagina)

From the weekly *Avanguardia*, issue 12, June 3, 1944

Lieutenant Juckeack, commander of V Company of II./1028 Grenadier Regiment: "The NCOs give the impression of being resolute and having fighting spirit; military conduct is rigid and disciplined. During inspections I always found the Italian SS positions to be ready for defense."

Lieutenant Manz, commander of II./1028 Grenadier Regiment: "During employment, up to this time collaboration with the Italian SS has been good. I found that orders that I gave have all been well executed. The conduct and discipline of the Italian soldiers are good. It is my duty to recognize their attitude toward difficulties and their military bearing. It should also be recognized that all soldiers and commanders are animated by a sincere fanaticism. All also show sincere camaraderie toward our soldiers. This is expressed above all by their readiness to assist our wounded."

Lieutenant Steutz, commander of VII Company of II./1028 Grenadier Regiment: "Cooperation has been excellent; there were absolutely no points of friction. The readiness for action on the part of officers, NCOs, and men has likewise also been equally excellent. In patrol actions and in defense against enemy attacks, they performed well. The military bearing of the officers was exemplary; NCOs and troops adjusted with the utmost passion to carry out German dispositions. Our Italian comrades in the trenches were always happy to fight and to work. As a quick judgment, I had the impression that the men of the Italian SS are the idealists of their people, who have the sad knowledge of betrayal and who tend to make up for the honor of Italy by the unreserved commitment of their life."

VIII. Conclusion

This battalion, which remained on the line without a break for more than sixty days, which carried out tasks that required boldness, valor, and continuous loss of life by all, held very difficult and key positions against which, in a vain attempt to break through the front, the overwhelming power of the enemy threw itself. This battalion, which replaced the red collar tabs of the Italian SS with the black collar tabs of the German SS, which inspired boundless admiration by all German officers under whom it served in combat, this battalion, the vanguard of the new Italian troops on the front, which never asked for anything but which gave its all (the radio and the press rarely mentioned it), which twice was mentioned in the German corps orders, has written one of the most beautiful pages of glory fully worthy of the highest martial traditions of the true Italy. Reconstituted, it will make itself talked about again.

Chapter VI
ITALIAN ARMED UNITS OF THE SS

SS-Gruppenführer Lothar Debes

Italian SS Legion soldiers training with a mortar, 1944

SS-Stubaf. Thaler with Waffen-Ostubaf. Giorleo

Following the reorganization of the brigade, the structure of the Italian volunteer legions (or Italian SS Legion) underwent major changes: it assumed the designation of Unità Armate Italiane delle SS (Italian Armed Units of the SS), while its staff was disbanded and absorbed by the Waffen-SS headquarters in Italy, which was operational beginning in July 1944 and led by SS-Gruppenführer Lothar Debes.[1] The inspectorate general commanded by Mannelli and Tschimpke continued to deal with the organization of various combat formations. For their exemplary performance demonstrated at Nettuno and for their fight against the rebels, the Germans decided to improve training of the new volunteers, with an eye toward employment at the front against the Allies.

A reserve headquarters was established, commanded by SS-Sturmbannführer Alois Thaler,[2] which had subordinate to it the units stationed at Cremona and the training camp at Rodengo-Saiano in the Brescia region. Thaler, who was a South Tyrolean, had fought with the SS Nord division in Finland, then on the Russian front, where he had lost a leg. He was able to walk with the aid of an artificial leg. He was summoned some months later to command the Italian SS Gruppo Pronto Intervento (Quick Reaction Group), also called the Compagnia zbV (Sonder Kompanie), which was a sort of special unit to be employed in hotspots at the front. Officers and NCOs were ordered to go to Waffen-SS schools in Germany and in occupied Europe for training. Between

From the left: SS-Obf. Erich Tschimpke, Stubaf. Asvero Gravelli, Generalmajor Piero Mannelli, and SS-Stubaf. Thaler. *Corbatti*

SS-Oberführer Otto Jungkunz during an operation, with several Italian officers

SS-Oberführer Otto Jungkunz interrogating captured partisans along with Italian officers

May and July 1944, sixty Italian volunteers from the officers' battalion attended a course at the SS-Panzergrenadierschule in Kleinschlag, Bohemia. About twenty other officers were sent to the SS artillery school in Beneschau, near Prague. A group of officers, mainly alpine officers, attended a specialization course at the engineer school in Dresden. A group of NCOs were sent to the SS und Waffen-Unterführerschule Lauenburg in Pomerania, where they received combat training and met with their Estonian, Lithuanian, French, and Dutch comrades. Other NCOs were sent to the SS und Waffen-Unterführerschule Laibach in Ljubljana. In May 1944, the Grenadier Brigade underwent further transformation. On May 10, command of the unit's headquarters was assumed by SS-Oberführer Otto Jungkunz,[3] previously chief of staff at the headquarters. The structure of the two regiments was reduced to only two battalions, with the addition of a cannon company for each of them.

Waffen-Grenadier-Regiment der SS 1 was commanded by Standartenführer Peghini, while Waffen-Grenadier-Regiment der SS 2 was under command of Standartenführer Enzo Celebrano.

The Fight against the Partisan Bands

The Waffen Grenadier Brigade der SS, while still involved in the training and organization of personnel in view of its employment in the front lines until October 1944, was engaged in fighting against partisan bands, especially in Piedmont, after which it was transferred to the province of Como, where the men could resume their training. During the period it spent in Piedmont, the Italian SS units were used as a garrison force to secure the territory as well as in many antipartisan operations, such as Habicht (in Val Sangone), Strassburg (in Valli di Lanzo), and Nachtgall (in the Pellice, Germanasca, Chisone, and Susa valleys); the last of these operations not only served to eliminate the main rebel bands but also ensured the control of the alpine passes with France, of vital importance in the event of enemy landings along the French or Ligurian coasts. In all these operations, the SS units operated along with other units of the RSI and with German units. The Debica also actively participated in the fight against the partisans; as of September 7, 1944, the unit assumed the new designation of Waffen-Fusilier Bataillon der SS Debica and was commanded by Hauptmann der Schutzpolizei Friederich Noweck,[4] previously the liaison officer with the unit. As of August 24, 1944, command of the brigade was assumed by SS-Obersturmbannführer Constantin Heldmann, previously commander of the heavy-weapons detachment of the Italian SS Legion. Promoted to *SS-Standartenführer* on November 9, 1944, he remained in command of the Italian SS formation until the end of the war.

Hauptmann der Schutzpolizei Friederich Noweck

Legionnaire Aldo Puliti during Operation Strassburg, carried out by Kampfgruppe Noweck in the Valli di Lanzo in September 1944, which led to the complete destruction of partisans operating in the area. *Magrini*

The order of September 7, 1944, also defined a new order of battle for the Italian SS Brigade:

Stab der Brigade
Waffen-Grenadier-Regiment der SS 81 (Italienische Nr.1)
    Stabskp., Inf.Gesch.Kp., I Bataillon, II Bataillon

Waffen-Grenadier-Regiment der SS 82 (Italienische Nr.2)
    Stabskp., Inf.Gesch.Kp., I Bataillon, II Bataillon

Waffen-Artillerie-Regiment der SS 59
    Stabsbatterie, I.Abteilung, II.Abteilung

Waffen-Panzerjäger-Abteilung der SS 59
    Stab, 1.(schwere) Batterie, 2.Batterie, 3.Batterie

Waffen-Fusilier-Bataillon der SS 59 'Debica'
Waffen-Pionier-Kompanie der SS 59
Waffen-Nachrichten-Kompanie der SS 59
Waffen-Sanitäts-Kompanie der SS 59
Waffen-Versorgungs-Regiment der SS59
Waffen-Feldersatz-Bataillon der SS 59

Transfer to the Como Region

The move of the Italian SS units to the province of Como was supposed to enable training of the personnel to be continued, but it also entered into the plans of the German high command to form a new defensive line long the Po and Ticino Rivers. At any rate, in early October 1944, Kesselring, commander of the German forces in Italy, had sent a telex to all military headquarters in Italy to include the Italian SS Brigade, ordering the resumption of operations against the partisan bands, whose activities continued to intensify. Resupply traffic was severely disrupted, and acts of sabotage were becoming ever more frequent. New operations were thus planned to eliminate the rebel bands in Lombardy and Piedmont. The Italian SS troops took part with four combat groups in various operations: Berni in Valsassina with the I./81, Avanti in Val d'Ossola and Strassburg in the Valli di Lanzo with Kampfgruppe Noweck, and another operation in the province of Bergamo with Kampfgruppe Celebrano and Degli Oddi. The Debica took part in Operation Vorwarts from October 9 to November 6, against partisan forces in the so-called Republic of Val d'Ossola. Operation Vorwarts resulted in dead, wounded, and prisoners on both sides. SS-Bataillon Debica carried out sweeps in towns and forests in Val Vigezzo up to the Swiss border along with men of the German police, Wehrmacht troops, three battalions of the GNR, and two companies of the Decima MAS. When the other formations returned, the Italian SS continued their sweeps in Val Formazza, in upper Val d'Ossola. Hauptmann Noweck was awarded the German Cross in Gold for the positive results achieved, on the basis of a citation written by SS-Brigdf. Willy Tensfeld, SS-und-Polizeiführer Oberitalien West, the highest decoration warded during the war to a member of the Italian SS Legion. Between late November and early December, pursuant to Kesselring's orders, new actions were undertaken to liberate the areas where partisan bands were still active.

The Italian SS Brigade, with two battalions—the I./81, under Stubaf. Paolo Comelli and the I./82, led by Stubaf. Emilio Bianchi—took part in an operation in the lower Valtellina along with units of the GNR, the Black Brigades, and a German *Gebirgsjäger* unit. This time the partisans suffered heavy losses, while those for the Italo-German units were minimal.

A company of the SS Brigade on the march. *Corbatti*

An SS volunteer in Valdossola

Debica troops during an antipartisan operation in Piedmont. *In the center,* Hstuf. Dal Dosso, the battalion commander. *Corbatti*

Mariano Comense, November 23, 1944: troops of the Italian SS Legion drawn up for the solemn ceremony. *Corbatti*

Ceremony at Mariano Comense

On November 23, 1944, a ceremony was held in a field on the road between Mariano Comense and Cantù, during which numerous awards were presented to the Italian volunteers, and the Silver Medal for Military Valor was awarded personally by Mussolini to the banner of the II./81 for valor shown on the Nettunia front. Presiding over the ceremony were Marshal Graziani, minister of defense of the RSI; SS-Obergruppenführer Karl Wolff, commander in chief of the SS and police in Italy; SS-Gruppenführer Lothar Debes, commander of the Waffen-SS in Italy; and SS-Brigadeführer Willy Tensfeld, commander of the SS and police in northwestern Italy.

New Operations

At the beginning of January 1945, a vast new operation (Hochland) was launched in the area of Valsesia and the province of Biella. The Italian SS Brigade employed a combat group consisting of some seven hundred men, drawn from the I. and II.82 along with a heavy-weapons detachment. The aim of the operation was to keep the partisans as far away as possible from the lines of communication between Lombardy and Piedmont, in view of the withdrawal of Italo-German troops east of the Ticino River. On January 30, the first phase of the operation ended with favorable results, but in early February a second phase was kicked off, designated Hochland Ost-West, along the eastern shore of Lake d'Orta. The Italian SS troops were employed mainly against the "Garibaldi" partisans. On February 14, 1945, a third phase began, with the two SS battalions engaged along the state road between Lake d'Orta and Lake Maggiore. On March 13, the operational cycle ended, during which the Italian SS volunteers had acquitted themselves well, as the German headquarters reported to SS-Standartenführer Heldmann.

Mariano Comense, November 23, 1944: Marshal Graziani, SS-Obergruppenführer Karl Wolff, and SS-Gruppenführer Lothar Debes inspect the Italian SS troops. *Corbatti*

Ostubaf. Armando Giorleo at the head of a combat group of the II./82 during an exercise on October 31, 1944, at Rodengo-Saiano. *Corbatti*

Mariano Comense, November 23, 1944: soldiers of the Italian SS Legion drawn up during the ceremony

Chapter VII
THE 29.WAFFEN-GRENADIER DIVISION DER SS

SS-Ostubaf. Heldmann

Waffen-Stubaf. Martinelli

Waffen-Stubaf. Paolo Comelli

The transformation of the brigade into a new SS division was officially authorized on February 10, 1945,[1] operational as of March 8, 1945, with divisional order number 1/45. All units received the identification number 29, previously assigned to another SS unit consisting of Russian anticommunist volunteers, the notorious Kaminski SS Brigade, which was disbanded before becoming a division, after having committed indescribable crimes during the repression of the Warsaw revolt in the summer of 1944. The new Italian 29th SS Division consisted of the following units and commanders:

29.Waffen-Grenadier-Division der SS (Italienische Nr.1)

Kdr: SS-Standartenführer Heldmann
Ia: SS-Sturmbannführer Georg Buchholz
Ib: SS-Obersturmführer Heinrich Tiemann
Ic: SS-Untersturmführer Georg Gerhard Unthan
Iva: SS-Hauptsturmführer Georg Pfaff
Feldgendarmerie: Waffen-Untersturmführer Spartaco Giongo
Stabs-Kompanie: SS-Obersturmführer Erwin Gödecke

Waffen-Gren.Rgt.d.SS 81 (Ital. Nr.1): Waffen-Ostubaf. Degli Oddi
I.Bataillon: Waffen-Sturmbannführer Paolo Comelli
II Bataillon Nettuno: Waffen-Sturmbannführer Remo Buldrini

Waffen-Gren.Rgt.d.SS 82 (Ital. Nr.2): Waffen-Standartenführer Enzo Celebrano
I.Bataillon: Waffen-Sturmbannführer Sergio Bianchi
II Bataillon: Waffen-Ostubaf. Armando Giorleo

Waffen-Artillerie Regiment der SS 29: Waffen-Sturmbannführer Carlo Pace
I.Abteilung: Waffen-Hauptsturmführer Giuliano Bini
II.Abteilung: Waffen-Hauptsturmführer Livio Ara

Waffen-Fusilier-Bataillon der SS 29 Debica: W-Hstuf. Dal Dosso, W-Hstuf. Premuda, W-Hstuf. Cantarella
Waffen-Panzerjäger-Abteilung der SS 29 (gemischte): W-Stubaf. Martinelli
Waffen-Pionier-Kompanie der SS 29: SS-Hauptsturmführer Rolf Lochmüller
Waffen-Nachrichten-Kompanie der SS 29: Waffen-Hstuf. Giovanni Moioli
Waffen-Versorgungs-Regiment der SS 29: Waffen-Stubaf. Giovanni Fratini
Waffen-Sanitäts-Kompanie der SS 29: Waffen-Hauptsturmführer Roberto Ofner
Waffen-Veterinär-Kompanie der SS 29: Waffen-Hauptsturmführer Aldo Guidi
Waffen-Feldersatz-Kompanie der SS 29: Waffen-Hstuf. Fausto Catasta
Offizierschule der italienischen Waffenverbände der SS: Waffen-Ostubaf. Tibero Bedotti

The division structure included a work battalion consisting of volunteers not suitable for combat duty. A company of this unit was transferred to the 24th SS Division in Friuli in March 1945. In early April 1945, the I Battalion of the 82nd Regiment was disbanded. Its place was to be taken by the battalion that was training at Rodengo-Saiano, but the unit was still training at end of the war, and the men were integrated into Kampfgruppe Thaler. The II Battalion of the 81st Regiment assumed the name Nettuno after a silver medal had been awarded to its battalion standard on November 23, 1944.

Kampfgruppe Binz

At the end of January 1945, with the Allies now only a few kilometers from the Po valley and Milan, Feldmarschall Kesselring ordered SS-Ogruf. Wolff to organize a new combat group with men of the 29.SS, to continue to protect the lines of communication, both from partisan attacks and any attacks by Allied troops themselves. The two Italian SS battalions that had fought on the Lazio front were chosen; the Debica and the Nettuno, which along with other Italian SS troops were used to constitute Kampfgruppe Binz, named for the German commander who led it, SS-Obersturmbannführer Siegfried Binz.[2] The various units of the *Kampfgruppe* completed their move to new positions in mid-February 1945. In particular, the I./WGR 81 Debica assumed positions in Val Nure, and II./WGR 81 Nettuno in Val Trebbia. Binz set up his headquarters in Piacenza. Subsequently, other RSI and several German units were subordinated to Kampfgruppe Binz, among them two companies of the Leonessa Armored Group, the Mameli Volunteer Battalion, the 2nd Company of the XXIII Pippo Astori Black Brigade, some personnel of the 630th GNR Provincial Headquarters in Piacenza, the Mantova Battalion of the V Mobile Alpine Black Brigade Quagliata, and II./Inf.Rgt. 329 of the 162.(turk) Infanterie.Division. On the other side, the partisans had begun to attack garrisons defended by Binz troops beginning in early February, severely testing the Italo-German forces. Some garrisons were surrounded by partisan forces, such as the one at Bettola in Val Nure, defended by 2./WGR 81, which had to be abandoned after two failed relief operations. The garrison at Passo Penice in Val Trebbia was defended by roughly thirty men from the 8.Kompanie of Oscha. Mario Sassone was also attacked by a partisan formation consisting of at least three hundred men. It was only after the intervention by a relief column that the threat could be eliminated. To respond to enemy provocations, Binz ordered a series of sweeps, employing mainly Italian SS troops. Other bitter engagements ensued against the rebel forces. In early April, in anticipation of a new withdrawal north of the Po River, some garrisons were abandoned, and the *Kampfgruppe* subsequently occupied a new defensive line in an attempt to contain enemy forces coming from Parma There was a contemporaneous resumption of partisan attacks. On April 20, Debica was still holding in the valleys of the Nure; the legionnaires had dug trenches, emplaced guns, and created obstacles to slow down the Allies, who had already reached Parma. The Nettuno had dug in at Rivergaro, 12 miles (20 km) south of Piacenza, with the mission of impeding partisan bands from coming into the valley.

Binz, wearing the Schutzpolizei uniform. *WAST*

Volunteers of 2.Kompanie of I./81 Debica, garrisoned at Bettola. The company was engaged in tough fighting against partisan bands between February 21 and 23, 1945. *Corbatti*

Nearing the End

A new operation designated Mughetto was undertaken in Val Camonica, in which the Italian SS participated with about three hundred men of II./82 along with the Tagliamento Blackshirt Legion and the 5th Quaglia Black Brigade; the operation was aimed at liberating the zone to ensure safe transit of German columns toward the Tonale Pass and the alpine valleys of the Alta Valtellina. In the Brescia area, the Italian SS Quick Reaction Group led by Thaler continued to fight and did so up to the end. On April 26, 1945, Thaler was ordered to organize the men of the training battalion at Rodengo–Saiano as a *Kampfgruppe* in order to try to reach the South Tyrol through the Tonale Pass.

Following brief fighting against partisan forces between April 26 and 27, which saw the withdrawal of the rebels, the three hundred men of Kampfgruppe Thaler began to move to the north on April 28. Near Sarnico, on Lake Iseo, they made contact with a partisan band; most of the Italian SS legionnaires chose to surrender, while Thaler and a faithful few managed to retreat to the mountains in the hopes of joining a fleeing German column. In the end, they were intercepted and had

Italian SS troops on parade following an exercise

Italian SS legionnaires emplacing a 47/32 antitank gun

A detachment of the Italian SS Legion on the march

to surrender to the partisan forces. Thaler was brought back to Rodengo-Saiano, where he was first shot and then, already dead, was also hanged.

In the Como region, all of the forces were put on alarm; Waffen-Standartenführer Enzo Celebrano, commander of Waffen-Grenadier-Regiment der SS 82, had sent out patrols throughout the Brianza area and along all of the roads that led to Lecco, Como, and Milan. The entire front was in movement, and the German headquarters on Lake Garda were pulling back. On April 26 at Alta Brianza, Celebrano signed the surrender of his garrison, and, following that, one by one, all of the various garrisons in Brianza and the Lecco area laid down their arms. Standartenführer Celebrano took leave of his men with the following words: "SS volunteers, we fall while still standing and with our weapons and with honor! We fought to redeem the honor of Italy! Force will not destroy what is right." On April 25, Ostubaf. Binz ordered his legionnaires to retreat, with the aim of reaching the Upper Adige, passing through Val Camonica. The bulk of the *Kampfgruppe* itself withdrew toward Erba in an attempt to join other troops of the division, as ordered by Heldmann. In the Piacenza area, the Italian personnel of the Binz continued to hold their positions, covering the retreat of other Italo-German units.

On April 26, the SS volunteers of Debica clashed with several American armored units and destroyed several enemy tanks with *Panzerfäuste*. The SS Debica and Nettuno Battalions continued to hold the two bridgeheads on the outskirts of Piacenza, while other men of the *Kampfgruppe* crossed the Po, not leaving until the twenty-eighth, when they also began to pull back to the north. Most of the troops surrendered to the Allied forces. The last battalion of the Italian Waffen-SS to lay down its arms was the II./82, led by Stubaf. Bianchi, while retreating toward the Tonale Pass. Many legionnaires were able to avoid capture, but many were captured by the partisans and summarily executed. Those who surrendered to the Anglo-American troops were interned in Allied concentration camps in Italy, mainly at Averso, Coltano, and Rimini.

Mariano Comense, April 26, 1945: trucks of the Todt organization made available to the division headquarters in order to transport the various SS units to Erba. *Corbatti*

A detachment of the Italian SS division on the march during a withdrawal

CHAPTER VIII
ITALIAN VOLUNTEERS IN THE KARSTJÄGER DIVISION

On the left: Karstjäger Division of 4.schwere.Kompanie engaged in a sweep in the Gorizia area, 1944. *On the right*: a group of Karstjäger with an MG34, engaged in a firefight against the partisans. *Corbatti*

Karstjäger conducting a sweep in the mountains

As already referred to in a preceding chapter, as early as the day after September 8, 1943, Italian volunteers had been recruited into the SS-Karstwehr-Bataillon, used as drivers, guides, and interpreters. When the order came in July 1944 to transform the unit into a new SS division,[1] the 24.Waffen Gebirgs-Karstjäger Division der SS, it was decided to extend enlistment to volunteers of all ethnic groups present in the Adriatsches Küstenland, the occupation zone along the Adriatic littoral. This resulted in a Waffen-Einheiten der SS unit; that is to say, a division consisting of non-German personnel.

This transformation was also to have entailed substitution of the double runes on the right collar tab by a symbol characteristic of the place of origin of the personnel; that is, the *Karstdiestel*, a plant typical of the Karst Plateau. However, this insignia was worn only rarely, since the German personnel preferred to continue to wear the double runes. A special Waffen-Ausbildungs-und-Ersatz-Bataillon was established for the integration of new recruits, with its headquarters at Ugovizza. At the end of July 1944, five hundred new volunteers arrived, among which were many natives of Friuli and Istria, along with Slovenes, Croats, and some Ukrainians. In February 1945, another four hundred volunteers arrived, once again mostly Italians along with 170 Spaniards. These data reflect the fact that the Italians represented the most numerous "foreign" contingent in the division after the Germans and Volksdeutschen.[2] The Italian volunteers were assigned to almost all of the various subunits of the division. These volunteers came from the recruitment centers along the Adriatic littoral; most opted to enlist in RSI units and in German formations. Those who chose to expressly enlist in the Waffen-SS were assigned to the Karstjäger. Among the Italian officers in the division, we have already mentioned the captain of the alpine corps, Giuseppe Ocelli. In the summer

Cividale del Friuli, February 1945. The three platoon leaders of the *Panzerkompanie* in front of an Italian P.40 tank. *From the right*, SS-Oscha. Cavagna, SS-Uscha. Dufke, and SS-Ustuf. Walter. *Corbatti*

A Karstjäger Division resupply column, with carts and mules, crossing a river

of 1944, with the rank of *Waffen-Hauptsturmführer der SS*, he served as an officer at the division headquarters. Later, he assumed command of one of the four companies of the Waffen-Ausbildugs-und-Ersatz-Bataillon, consisting of Italian, Slovene, and Croat volunteers, ending the war with the rank of *Waffen-Sturmbannführer der SS*. Among the other Italian officers who joined the division between summer and autumn of 1944, we would note Dr. Franco Narducci, a medical officer at division headquarters with the rank of *Waffen-Sturmbannführer der SS*, who earlier had served at the Waffen-SS hospital in Prague. Within the *Panzerkompanie*, commanded by SS-Ostuf. Behrend, was Waffen-Hauptsturmführer der SS Pistocchi in the deputy commander slot.

Waffen-Obersturmführer der SS Odorico Borsatti[3] was in command of the Reiter-Zug (cavalry platoon), while Waffen-Untersturmführer der SS Fabrizi led a platoon of 4.Kompanie of I./59. The Karstjäger never reached the level of a fully manned division, and on December 5, 1944, by new order of the SS-FHA, it was downgraded to brigade status, designated the Waffen-Gebirgs (Karstjäger) Brigade der SS. The German headquarters had banked on an influx of a large number of "non-German" volunteers from the Adriatic littoral, but that did not happen. The lack of cadre, officers, and NCOs in sufficient numbers sealed its fate. On September 20, 1944, the unit had a strength of twenty-seven officers,103 NCOs, and 1,799 soldiers, for a total of 1,989 men. In November of that year, the effective strength rose to 2,479 men, still too few to form a division.

On February 10, 1945, the units was once again transformed as a division, but still at a minimal level, since the effective strength never rose above three thousand. Despite the naming of two new divisional commanders in succession, SS-Ostubaf. Karl Marcks and SS-Ostubaf. Wagner, neither of whom ever officially joined the unit, in the field the 24.SS remained under command of SS-Stubaf. Werner Hahn[4] until the end of the war. In the face of a serious lack of personnel, the division found itself consisting of a single Gebirgsjäger regiment, Waffen-Gebirgsjäger-Regiment der SS 59, initially with three battalions

Odorico Borsatti, in an early 1944 photo, still in the Italian uniform with the RSI insignia and with the gladio on a white background for cavalry units. *Corbatti*

Bandenkampfabzeichen in silver

A Karstjäger machine gun team in combat. *Corbatti*

SS-Ostuf. Helmuth Prasch, awarded the Bandeskampfabzeichen in Gold. *TKS 24*

(then reduced to two), a single artillery battery, an armored company, a medical company, and various support units. The men were scattered over various localities in Friuli, engaged in antipartisan operations, with excellent results. Reflecting the valor they demonstrated in the field in the fight against the partisans, many members of the division were awarded the Bandenkampfabzeichen, the badge for fighting the partisans.[5]

It was only at the end of the war, between late April and early May 1945, that the last personnel of the division were engaged against Allied regular troops in an attempt to block the British and New Zealand units that were attempting to enter the Reich through the Tarvisio and Monte Croce Carnico (Plöckenpass) passes. The Gebirgsjäger SS continued to fight to the death, armed to the teeth. In fact, they did not lay down their arms until May 9, 1945, near the border of Tarvisio in the area comprising Arnoldstein and Hermagor in Lower Carinthia. The fate of the Italians in the division was particularly tragic, especially those who sought to return to their homes in territories occupied by the Communist partisans. Many of them ended up in the sinkholes in the karst or shot by improvised peoples' tribunals after summary trials. It was a sad end after years of terrible and bitter fighting.

Cover of the weekly *Adria Illustrierte* of April 21, 1945, with a member of 4.SS-Feldhundstaffel, the unit that had German shepherd dogs trained for antipartisan actions and used to hunt down partisans

CHAPTER IX

SS-POLIZEI-REGIMENT BRIXEN

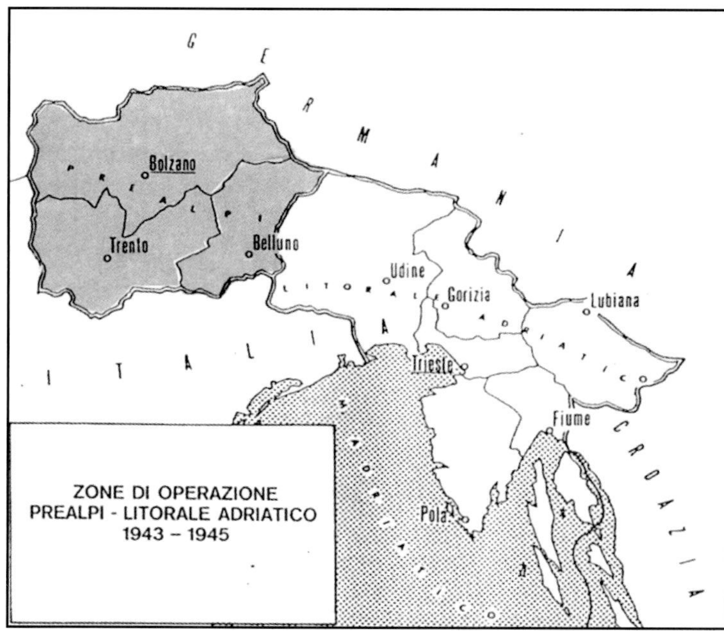

Gauleiter Franz Hofer inspecting a unit in the Tyrol

Members of the Brixen pose for a photo. *Baratter*

Following the German occupation of Italian territory after September 8, the provinces of Bolzano, Trento, and Belluno were united into the Operationszone Alpenvorland (Alpine Occupation Zone) under German political and military control. Franz Hofer, previously *Gauleiter* (governor) of the Tyrol, was designated as supreme commissar of the zone. As early as October 1, 1943, orders were issued for the formation of South Tyrolean police units for the maintenance of order in the various provinces. To that end, a nucleus of 250 German police NCOs were provided. Naturally, the Germans hoped for an influx of recruits on a "voluntary" basis, but in the end they had to resort to forced conscription.[1] The Brixen (Bressanone) was formed by order of the chief of the Ordnungspolizei by letter dated October 12, 1944: "A regiment must be formed, having a nucleus of German personnel and completed with Germans from the South Tyrol. The regiment will be called the SS-Polizei-Regiment Brixen."

In a communique sent on September 20, 1944, by the highest police authorities in Alpenvorland to Hofer and the supreme commander of the SS and the police for Italy, the date differs: "On October 15, a new police regiment will be formed in Bressanone with a strength of about two thousand men." To that end, a long list of materials were requested to equip the new unit: more than two thousand steel helmets, shirts, long cloth pants, overcoats, jackets, corduroy pants, wool gloves, etc. With respect to armament, two thousand rifles, eight light-grenade launchers, four heavy-grenade launchers, and hand grenades, all of which were of Italian origin. South Tyroleans who enlisted in the unit opted for German citizenship, while Italians and a small group of Ladini[2] opted for Italian citizenship. Training was carried out in the South Tyrol from October 1944 until February 1945. The regiment's order of battle included three battalions, each of four companies. The fourth heavy-weapons company of each battalion consisted of a machine gun platoon, a mortar platoon, and an antitank platoon. Each battalion had a signals platoon. There was also a motorized column for resupply.

The unit had the following *Feldpost* numbers: *Regimentsstab*: 31464; I Battalion: 01773; II Battalion: 18524; II Battalion: 05010. The regiment's cadre were for the most part Germans, but there were also South Tyrolean personnel. Oberst der Schutzpolizei Ernst Korn was appointed as regimental commander. He had previously been commander of the Ordnungspolizei in Albania. The battalion commanders were Hauptmann Boogest, Hauptmann Heinz Opitz, and Major Beussel.

The Day of the Oath

The swearing in of the Brixen was scheduled for late February 1945 and was to be administered by Gauleiter Hofer. Unfortunately, the day chosen for the ceremony turned out to be rather cold and rainy; an incredible winter rainstorm raged over Bressanone, and the poor members of Brixen were left for hours in the pouring rain waiting for the arrival of the *Gauleiter*, who was very late in coming. As Alois Pfeiffer[3] wrote, "It rained. Since

Members of a South Tyrol Polizei regiment during a training march. *Baratter*

Members of a German police unit in Italy, autumn 1944

the morning we had lined up in the courtyard of the barracks: the swearing-in was supposed to be in the morning with Gauleiter Hofer. Instead, the swearing-in took place in the afternoon; without eating we had to stay on standing waiting for Hofer until he finally arrived. We were shivering, the wind was blowing, we were in a bad way. Standing there for hours and hours."

When Hofer finally got there, the oath was read: "I swear to you, Adolf Hitler, Führer and Chancellor of the Reich, fealty and courage. I solemnly promise you and to my superiors designated by you obedience unto death, may God help me." At that point, two thousand soldiers were to shout in unison "*Ich schwöre!*," but everyone remained in absolute silence. The officers began to get nervous, glaring at the men in the first rank, but no one so much as drew breath. The only sound to be heard was the rain beating upon the ground. The testimony of one of the few survivors[4] follows: "At five in the evening the supreme commissar arrived. He made a speech that seemed to never end, and then we were to take the oath. He read the text of the oath. We were really bitter. No one opened their mouth! Everyone remained silent." Faced with that terrible impasse, someone got the idea that the men had not understood well how they were supposed to act, so, exhorted by Hofer himself, Oberstleutnant Korn gave a quick briefing on the ritual of the oath. The oath was repeated, but once again everyone remained silent. Hofer and most of the officers present were stunned and so full of rage that they ordered all the men to be stripped of their weapons and to be sent to their barracks, to be confined there. The idea of not swearing the oath, according to some, was floating among the men for some days prior to the ceremony, as Alois Pfeiffer[5] again refers: "Within the regiment the idea not to swear the oath had circulated for several days, from one to another . . . because we were treated so badly." The testimony of Peter Pöder[6] ran along the same lines: "We already knew what the fate of the Hitler regime would be; certainly Hitler was refused from the political point of view, but there were also many young South Tyroleans present who refused because of their inner religious convictions. I think that it can be stated that the refusal to take the oath happened both for political and religious motives."

Elements of a South Tyrol police regiment in action

A South Tyrolean police regiment on a parade field. *Baratter*

Gauleiter Franz Hofer, from a period calendar

Hofer with German officers at the Bolzano station

Gustav Lombard, in the photo with *Standartenführer* rank insignia, during the ceremony for the award of the Knight's Cross in March 1944

Transfer to the Eastern Front

What then was to be done with these "rebels"? Surely, two thousand men could not be shot, so it was thought to punish them in another way: send them far from their lands and transfer them en bloc to the Eastern Front. It was in fact decided to send them to the front in Silesia, in the area southeast of Breslau, where Soviet forces were making deep advances. In March 1945, a train convoy of cattle cars left the Upper Adige with two thousand soldiers on board, bound for the front in Silesia, directly on the front lines. They were offloaded in Hirschberg to be integrated into the 31.SS-Frw.Gr.Division.[7] The division, commanded by SS-Brigadeführer Gustav Lombard, had been formed in October 1944, in the Hungarian Batschka region with the remnants of 23.Waffen-Grenadier-Division der SS Kama, *volksdeutsche* Hungarians and other personnel coming from the Balkan region. After having protected the evacuation of the German population from the Batschka, the division was engaged first in southern Hungary and then in the Lake Balaton region.

From there it was pulled back to the Maribor region in Styria, to be reorganized. In late January 1945, returned to operational status, it was sent to Silesia, in the Hirschberg area, as a reserve for Heeresgruppe Mitte. Subordinated to 4.Panzer-Armee, it saw combat in the Liegnitz, Goldberg, and Jauer sectors against Soviet forward forces. In early March, SS-Polizei-Regiment Brixen arrived as a replacement for its third "lost" regiment, SS-Frw.Gren.Regiment 80. Some of the cadre of the South Tyrolean regiment were also assigned to other units of the same division to make up for losses suffered by the division in previous engagements. The new SS-Frw. Gren.Regiment 80 was often designated as SS-Regiment Schön, named for the new regimental commander, SS-Stubaf. Rudolf Schön. The regimental adjutant was SS-Ostuf. Moeller. Commanding I Battalion was SS-Stubaf. Helmuth Ganz.[8] The men of SS-Frw.Gren.Regiment 80 moved to the area east of Striegau, northeast of Hirschberg, to relieve Infanterie-Regiment 337 of the 208.Inf.Div. (led by Oberst Lothar Berger). Oberstleutnant Albinus, commander of Inf.Rgt.337, thus describes the relief operation:[9] "Inf.Rgt. 237, until that time located in the Saaru Haidau sector facing north, was relieved during the night of March 5 by Regiment Schön of 31.SS-Division. That unit was a Tyrolean police unit consisting of Ladins commanded by German cadre. The Ladins had been torn from their alpine valleys. For many of them, it was the first time that they had ever been on a train. We didn't know what they were doing in this area. . . . They were not given their weapons until the operation began. Strong rear guards of our unit remained in position until March 7, with the 'honest' Ladins to avoid any disasters if the Soviets attacked. Thank God that did not happen." But the odyssey of the South Tyrolean volunteers was only beginning. At home they had been trained with Italian weapons, while on the Silesian front they were given German weapons, which they had never seen before, let alone used. When they made contact with Soviet soldiers and began actual combat, there were many defections.

Some quickly raised their hands, as a sign of surrender, but were killed anyway in the heat of battle, while others, seized by panic, did not even get to shoot, such as Luis Gögele:[10] "I remember at a certain point, on the front line, I saw Russians running in the trenches, and I could have shot them but I didn't do so because I thought that even there there would have been a mother who cried." But not everyone acted that way. Many soldiers, having grasped the seriousness of the situation and motivated above all by wanting to save their skins, fought as best as they could, quickly learning the hard lessons of war on the Eastern Front. SS-Regiment Schön participated along with Inf.Rgt.337 in the recapture of Striegau. Oberst Berger, taking into account the inexperience of the South Tyrolean conscripts, put them in the defense of a sector outside the city and only when Soviet resistance began to slack off brought them into the fighting. Schön's troops were later employed to secure the city from further possible enemy counterattacks. On March 16, SS-Frw.Gren. Regiment 80 was relieved from the Muhrau-Saarau sector again by Inf.Rgt.337 and, after a brief pause at Striegau, was shifted to another threatened sector of the front, between Löwenberg and Goldberg, farther to the northwest, and then to the sector between Lang-Neuendorf-Wolfsdorf. The regimental command post was set up at Neukirch. The Soviets attacked the sector defended by the regiment with many tanks, forcing the SS grenadiers to withdraw to west of the village of Sussenbach, where a key crossroads had to be defended. The enemy was finally halted there; many tanks were destroyed there by *Panzerfaust* rounds, and a new defensive front was established. Sussenbach was retaken shortly afterward, while Neukirch was definitively left in enemy hands. During this fighting, SS-Frw.Gren.Regiment 80 suffered heavy losses. In late March, a new defensive line was established south of Harpersdorf and Steinberg. 31.SS-Division remained in these positions until the end of April, when it was relieved. What remained of SS-Frw.Gren.Regiment 80 was parceled out to the division's other two regiments. After having been engaged in the Strehlen sector, the division pulled back to the Königgratz region, where it was completely surrounded by the Soviets. Those who were not killed by enemy fire were captured and sent off to Siberia. Only a few survivors of the Brixen returned from the Soviet concentration camps after the war, and in an ironic twist, they were those who held Italian identity documents.

Map of Silesia, with locations underlined where troops of the South Tyrolean regiment of the 31.SS were in action

Soldiers of 31.SS on the march on the Silesian front, March 1945

German troops during a withdrawal on the Silesian front, 1945

Waffen-SS soldiers engaged against Soviet tanks on the Eastern Front

Germany, September 1944. Young Waffen-SS recruits take the oath on their commander's sword.

CHAPTER X
BROTHERS IN ARMS: GIORGIO AND GUIDO GARDINI

Münsingen, October 1943: SS-Stubaf. Alois Thaler speaking with Major Guido Fortunato. *Corbatti*

A rifle company of the first Ausbildungsbataillon on the march. *Corbatti*

Italian SS Legion mortarmen on the march. *AC*

Guido Giardini was born in Gubbio in 1924. His brother Giorgio was born the following year. Immediately upon the formation of the new government of the Italian Social Republic, both brothers entered the Guardia Nazionale Repubblicana (Republican National Guard) officers' school at Fontanello, near Parma. In September 1944, Guido and Giorgio completed their courses and were promoted to the rank of officer candidates. They then joined the Waffen-SS, enlisting at the Cremona recruitment office along with other officer cadets from the GNR school at Fontanello, among whom were Alessandro Gubiotti, Gianpietro Amgeletti, Pietro Zoppia, and Aldo Scavizzi. They were then sent to the Cremona recruit center, where the commander was their own father, Waffen-Ostubaf. Orazio Gardini.[1] The two brothers initially were given the rank of *Waffen-Uscha*, before becoming *Waffen-Standartenoberjunker*[2] a month later. In early 1945 they were promoted to *Waffen-Ustuf. der SS* along with the other former GNR cadets. Waffen-Ustuf. Giorgio Gardini was later designated as adjutant of the Cremona recruit battalion, while Guido Gardini became a *Zugführer* (platoon leader) in Sonderkompanie, or Compagnia Pronto Intervento (quick-reaction company), a special unit under direct orders of SS-Stubaf. Alois Thaler, commander of the Italian SS replacement and training detachment.

SS volunteers training at Rodengo-Saiano; note the use of camouflage tent material. *Corbatti*

In November 1944, Guido Gardini, as a *Zugführer* in the Sonderkompanie, was sent to San Donato Piacentino, south of the Po front, for an antipartisan action that lasted until the end of January 1945, when his unit returned to Cremona. On January 21, Allied planes bombed the Cremona SS barracks, killing six Italian SS men and wounding many others. Among the wounded was the younger Gardini brother, who was sixteen years old and had enlisted in the Italian SS in late October 1944. Following the bombing, all the replacement units still in Cremona were sent to Rodengo-Saiano in the province of Brescia, where the SS training battalion was stationed. In March 1945, a new training battalion was formed, slated to become the new I./82 when its formation was completed, in April 1945. That same month, all the men of this new battalion, including the Gardini brothers, received the black SS collar tabs. Waffen-Ustuf. Guido Gardini became the 81 mm mortar platoon *Zugführer* in the 4th Heavy-Weapons Company of the battalion, commanded by Waffen-Ostuf. Bruno Tamponi. At the same time, Waffen-Ustuf. Giorgio Gardini was designated as *Zugführer* in the battalion's 1st Company, led by Waffen-Ostuf. Savoi. The 1st Company included about fifty Italian and Spanish volunteers coming from the 28.Frw.Gr.Div. Wallonien. The Spaniards had served previously in the famous Division Azul on the Leningrad front and were led by their countryman, Waffen-Oscha. Camargo.

Cremona, October 1944. The Quick-Reaction Company parading through the city streets on the occasion of the visit of the plenipotentiary of the Third Reich in Italy, Otto Rahn. In the forefront, Uscha. Guido Gardini. Behind him, wearing a *Feldmütze*, is the company commander, Ostuf. Michele Lombardo. *Corbatti*

On the right, seated, is Ustuf. Giorgio Gardini, still wearing the rank of cadet sergeant, with Oscha. Camargo, commander of the Spanish group attached to the Italian SS Legion. *Corbatti*

Rodengo-Saiano: *from the left,* Tschimpke, Thaler, Giorleo, and other officers watching an exercise of Italian troops

Because of the chaotic situation at the front, the new I./82 was unable to join the rest of 29.SS.Division prior to the war's end. On April 26, 1945, the commander of the Italian SS replacement and training detachment, SS-Stubaf. Thaler, and the commandant of the recruit depot, Waffen-Ostubaf. Oreste Gardini, were ordered to organize their best troops into a combat group, known as Kampfgruppe zbV or Kampfgruppe Thaler, with the aim of reaching the South Tyrol via the Tonale Pass. After a brief firefight between April 26 and 27 at Rodengo-Saiano, during which the partisans were rebuffed, the three hundred men of Kampfgruppe Thaler began to move north during the day on April 28. They were, however, immediately stalled at Sarnico on Lake Iseo by a partisan band. Most of the Italian personnel surrendered after the partisans promised them that they would not be executed. SS-Stubaf. Thaler, along with all the German personnel and a few Italian volunteers, decided not to trust them and continued to make their way fighting. What was left of the *Kampfgruppe* then managed to make it to the mountains, where Thaler and his men hoped to join a German column that was headed to the South Tyrol. But that did not happen, and Thaler and his group were captured by another partisan formation. Thaler was brought back to Rodengo-Saiano, where he was brutally executed.

SS-Stubaf. Alois Thaler. *Corbatti*

The thirteen Italian officers who had stayed with the *Kampfgruppe* were also captured; among them were Waffen-Ostubaf. Oreste Gardini and his two sons Guido and Giorgio. All were condemned to death, and in fact a local newspaper reported their execution on April 29, 1945. The news, however, proved to be unfounded, because on May 2 these officers were saved from being executed thanks to the arrival of an Italian unit attached to the Allies, which took them into custody. They were then moved to the camp at Coltano, near Pisa, where they remained several months. Waffen-Ustuf. Gianpietro Angeletti died in captivity because of the miserable conditions of the camp at Coltano. When Giorgio and Guido Gardini were released from that camp, they were arrested by order of the Italian government and sentenced to several years in prison. Their father, Oreste Gardini, who had commanded a Blackshirt battalion prior to September 8 and had served during the early months of the RSI as the GNR territorial commander in the province of Ancona, was sentenced to a long period of incarceration. There were another two members of the Gardini family in the Italian Waffen-SS: Waffen-Uscha. Arolodo Gardini, who served with the supply detachment of the recruit department, and SS-Grenadier Giancarlo Gardini, who served with the recruit battalion. Giancarlo was badly wounded during an aerial bombing of Cremona and died in October 1945 due to the wounds he had suffered.

Mariano Comense, November 23, 1944. Marshal Graziani attaching the Silver Medal for Military Valor to the standard of II./ Waffen-Grenadier-Regiment der SS 81, which would later be designated as the Nettuno.

Chapter XI

PIO FILIPPANI-RONCONI

Waffen-Obersturmführer Filippani-Ronconi. Note the special collar tab with three arrows on the uniform.

German infantry attacking on the Anzio front, 1944

Pio Alessandro Carlo Fulvio Filippani-Ronconi was born in Madrid on March 10, 1920, to a noble Roman family. He returned to Italy, where he continued his studies in Rome at the San Giuseppe de Merode secondary school, where his philosophy professor saw a future for him as a bright student. He then attended the university in Rome, where, in addition to obligatory courses in Greek and Latin humanities, he took courses in oriental religions, achieving the highest grades possible. He was almost obsessed with oriental languages and studied Sanskrit, Turkish, Persian, Arabic, Tibetan, Chinese, and many others. His knowledge of these languages paid for his studies: he read the radio news in these foreign languages. With the onset of the Second World War, he joined the University Volunteer Company and was integrated into the 3rd Sardinian Grenadier Regiment, choosing to join its Arditi platoon, fighting in Libya, where he was wounded. On September 8, 1943, he was in Cancello Arnone in the province of Caserta with the 180th Infantry Regiment, where he was again wounded during an Allied bombing raid. He refused to turn over his weapons to a group of Germans, preferring to level them against them, but then reaching a very cavalier "nonbelligerent" agreement. Immediately thereafter, he decided to continue to fight alongside his original ally. In 2005, we met with the professor at his home in Rome and asked him a number of questions regarding his experiences in the Waffen-SS.

How and when did you join the Waffen-SS?
At the SS headquarters of the Guardia del Duce, where all of the ministries of the new republic had moved. The Waffen-SS were selected personnel, reliable, who would have enchanted any youngster of those times. I had already fought in North Africa and was part of an Arditi unit. It was September 1943; I was an adjutant, with duties also as secretary to Undersecretary Barracu, but I was frankly bored of being inactive. We left a couple of weeks later by train.

How did the Germans behave toward the Italian volunteers?
At first very badly, but after the episode at Anzio they changed noticeably. In the Waffen-SS we were all equals, but not in the negative sense of the word; officers and soldiers had the same rights and the same duties.

Is it true that a special collar tab was created for the Italian Waffen-SS?
It was an idea of mine. We had a sort of competition among the officers to come up with a special collar tab for out unit. I came up with three arrows to symbolize the three characteristics of the human spirit: feeling, thought, and desire. The red tab symbolized the desire to shed our blood for the homeland.

Can you tell us something about your time at the Anzio bridgehead?
Ours was a war of position. We were hidden in the trenches amid water and mud. Patrols were organized to carry out raids behind enemy lines. On more than one occasion, I had to carry a wounded comrade on my shoulders to bring him back. I walked along the Via Appia; we had broken into the American defensive system. They were shooting at us; I dropped to the ground. I was in such a hurry that I didn't realize that I was surrounded by corpses. A German sergeant helped me carry a wounded soldier back to an aid station, but it was useless.

It wasn't the only time I brought wounded back to our lines. On another occasion, an enemy shell fragment hit me, and as a result of my actions, which I considered completely normal, I was awarded the Iron Cross Second Class. I was the first Italian to receive an award after the shameful events of September 8, and it was presented to me by Colonel Diebitsch, who informed Il Duce of it.

What kind of weapons were you equipped with?
It was a very mixed lot, and on the Anzio front we also used the preferred weapon of the Arditi, the dagger. I had already gained some experience with close-in fighting and had to teach both Italians and Germans—who had no such experience—how to get out of tight spots quickly and silently.

The Reasons for a Choice

Let us hear again from the professor about what some of the reasons were that led so many young Italians to join the Waffen-SS, excerpting from a text of his published in the magazine *Arthos*:[1] "Now let's get to the point. What made me and so many others choose the fighting SS?—that is, the Waffen-SS, a German militia of political origin, which at the time was becoming a true and proper European army. For me, there were at least three reasons: The 'Europeanness'; compared to the Flemings, Germans, Scandinavians, et al., we Italians could show that we were better in every sense and in every field.

The insignia with the three arrows for the collar tab

Tiger I tanks of schwere Panzer Abteilung 508 on the Anzio front, March 1944. *NA*

Italian SS Legion soldiers with a 47/32 antitank gun

An Italian SS detachment ready for inspection. *Taylor*

"In the second place, there was, and I am not exaggerating at all, the 'mystic' element of that primordial 'terribleness' of action united with an archaic concept of hierarchy, which meant that at the center of these fighting units there was an order, like that of the Teutonic Knights, that irresistibly attracted anyone who aspired to total dedication of self in combat. This overwhelming sense of devotion, of sacrificial offering of one's self, had grown from an esoteric strain of teaching, in part deriving from experiences of the various Thule-Gesellschaften after the First World War and, in part, from the meditative experiences brought to Europe from the various SS missions in Tibet in the late 1930s. Added to that was the runic symbol itself of the double 'runes' of victory, the two *Siegrunen* (from *Sieg*, 'victory'), which indicated the aspiration toward victory over one's self and over the world.

"A third reason, especially for a young officer such as myself, was that in the Waffen-SS it was possible, or at least so I believed, to experience personally the training and combat level of the German armed forces, governed down to the lowest levels by that *Auftragstaktik* by which everyone knew what they were supposed to do under any circumstances and situation, without having to wait for the prompting of superiors (the so-called *Befehlstaktik*)."

Wartime Experiences

"In November 1943, having taken my leave of the Gold Medal recipient Barracu, presidential undersecretary of the RSI, whose adjutant I was, I enlisted as a private in the first Waffen-SS that I ran across at Gargnano on Lake Garda, where Il Duce was living. Sent to Verona, where General Hansen was forming an Italian combat unit, I was reinstated in my rank as an officer and assigned to the 1st Company. I narrowly avoided becoming the adjutant to General Lombard, General Hansen's replacement. I was unaware that in the meantime, a number of Italian battalions had been created, some of which, coming from the camps at Münsingen in Württemberg and Debica in Moravia, had become part of the Waffen Miliz, later transformed into the Unità Armate Italiane delle SS (Italienische Freiwillige Legion, I.F.L.), from which was drawn the Italian 1a Brigata d'Assalto (Erste Sturmbrigade) of the Waffen-SS, constituted as a result of an agreement between Il Duce and the führer in October 1943. At this point, the true story of the so-called Italian SS begins, a term of convenience adopted to simplify recruitment of Italian personnel. In reality, as long as they wore red collar tabs, the soldiers of the Assault Brigade—prior to being employed at the front—were only auxiliary units of the proper Waffen-SS units. It was only after action at the front and the extraordinary displays of valor on the line did they become—with the black insignia on which the symbol of the three arrows within a circle, as an alternative to the *Siegrunen*—Waffen-SS for all intents. . . . The uniform was that of the Italian assault units (gray green in color): paratrooper smock without collar and ski trousers closed at the

Milan, Adriatica barracks, March 1944: men of the Degli Oddi Battalion parading before the authorities prior to leaving for the Nettunia front. *Corbatti*

calves; German alpine cap with the Totenkopf and the Roman eagle with fasce on the left of the cap, and the same on the smock; rank insignia for officers and NCOs were German on the shoulder; belt as worn by the German SS with the inscription '*Meine Ehre Heisst Treue*' ('My honor is loyalty'); the color of the tabs and the background for rank insignia was red for 'subordinate' units, *Waffen-Einheiten*, and black for personnel who were for all intents SS—SS-Einheiten, that is, those who had shown valor at the front and thus were proper SS, completely equivalent to the German SS. The battalion was readied on March 12, 1944, with a strength of 650 men, or thirty-two officers, ninety-three NCOs, and 525 other ranks, to which were added about a dozen 'clandestine' boys aged fourteen to sixteen, whom we tried to send back home or to the institutions from which they had escaped to come to fight. . . . Whether this was an assault unit or, as called for, a 'suicide unit' is shown by the words addressed to us by General Emilio Canevari at an official meeting, at the Biocca barracks, on the eve of our departure: 'Fellow officers, not one step back! You are not going to cut a fancy figure, but only to die! Your behavior will determine whether or not the Germans rearm an Italian army.' It was like throwing a pail of gasoline on a smoldering fire: barely armed and summarily equipped, we set off like avenging furies from Milan (Greco Station) on March 13, 1944, at 0700, for Littoria, where we arrived about a week later after a very slow journey while waiting for other units to form a *Kampfgruppe* under SS-Oberführer Diebitsch, units that never arrived because they were given other duties or were destroyed in action along the road to the south.

Milan, Adriatica barracks, March 1944: Ostubaf. Degli Oddi and Ostuf. Mincucci speaking with the widow of the *federale* of Milan, Aldo Resega, who presented the combat flame to the battalion, made by the women of the Republican Fascist party of Milan. *Corbatti*

A moment during the ceremony at Mariano Comense, November 1944

"The 1st Company, to which I belonged, under Captain Buldrini, entered the line near Cisterna, in the sector of II./SS-Panzer-Grenadier Rgt. 35, while the 2nd and 3rd Companies went to the Cisterna-Mussolini Canal and Borgo Podgora, in the sector held by II./SS-Panzer-Grenadier Rgt. 36; in particular, the 2nd Company relieved a company of the Barbarigo, which had suffered heavy losses. The muddy ground, with water 60 centimeters [2 ft.] below the surface, and the need to dig trenches, at night, for a war of position, made living conditions very difficult."

Recognition by Our Ally

"The II Battalion of the 81st Regiment, designated 'Degli Oddi,' was to my knowledge given official recognition on several occasions. The first, dated May 3, 1944, issued by the *Reichsführer-SS*, stated, 'For valor shown and for their sense of duty, the Italian SS volunteers are considered to be Waffen-SS personnel with all of the duties and all rights'; the second, again signed by the *Reichsführer-*

Rodengo-Saiano, October 31, 1944; SS-Obf. Tschimpke inspects the Ausbildungs-Bataillon during training. To his left, SS-Stubaf. Thaler, and behind him, Ostubaf. Giorleo and Ostuf. Filippani-Ronconi.

Marshal Graziani presenting the Silver Medal to the standard of II Battalion. *Corbatti*

Banner and standards of the Italian SS Legion, autumn 1944

SS, stated, 'For valor shown and for their sense of duty, the personnel of the Italian Waffen-SS shall wear rank and identification insignia with a black background completely identical to that worn by other SS personnel.' And finally, the third recognition of honor: 'Authorization is granted to change the designation of the First Assault Brigade of the Italian SS Legion to 1st Italian SS Grenadier Brigade.' In autumn 1944, at Mariano Comense, Marshal of Italy Rodolfo Graziani affixed the Silver Medal for Military Valor to the II Battalion standard. A German regiment, along with the 81st and 82nd Regiments of the 29th SS Division (Italian 1st), rendered the honors by parading before the 146 survivors of the fighting at Nettuno.

"The justification for the award was as follows: 'Along with the other vanguards of the new Italian troops at the front, it remained on the line uninterruptedly for more than two months, carrying out particularly difficult tasks and holding key positions against which, in vain, powerful enemy thrusts raged until the front was broken through. Twice mentioned in the Corps Orders, it was rewarded by being authorized to wear the black tabs of the German SS; it received German awards and numerous promotions for action in the face of the enemy. A shining example of faith and great love for the homeland, it resisted with inexorable tenacity and valor against the unequal and very bitter fight over many days, consecrating the oath with the blood of more than 70 percent of its men and writing one of the most beautiful pages of glory, worthy of the highest traditions of the true Italy. Nettuno Front—Rome, March 17—June 5, 1944, XXXII.'"

Professor Pio Filippani-Ronconi passed away on February 11, 2010.

Volunteer Giuseppe Vassalli of the II./82 in camouflage garb and armed with a Carcano 91/38 cavalry carbine

Chapter XII
GIUSEPPE VASSALLI: SS LEGIONNAIRE

Giuseppe Vassalli wearing the SS uniform

I never had the fortune to have personally met with Giuseppe Vassalli[1] when he was still alive, but over the last few years we have had many telephone conversations that were long and very interesting, from which many articles for our publications were written concerning his combat experience with the Waffen-SS. Giuseppe subsequently gathered his wartime memoirs in several books, distributed by our own cultural association. These writings will act as a reference point for all military history students and researchers relating to the subject of Italian volunteers in the Waffen-SS. Following are selected items written by Vassalli that have previously been published in our magazine.

Storm and Assault

"In 1943, when autumn was giving way to winter in Italy, many young men wandered about in the dark without really knowing of what kind of stuff they were made. A choice had to be made; a way had to be found to affirm their intellectual honesty. Maybe this fatal war, breaking the equilibrium of the old Europe, was paving the way for the flowering of new apparent truths that we did not even suspect at the time. Our first aim was to show the Germans that we were equal to them in battle. To show the Germans that we came from a mystical base, the Fascist mystique, and we wanted to reach the Nazi ethic with all of its components of *Geist*; that is, of spirit. We joined the Waffen-SS subconsciously or because they invited us to join. We did not enlist with our flags and our officers. We were not in the service of Germany but of our own people, and we were the European army defending the rights of Italy in the growing *Bund*, the federation of the 'States of Europe.' As the European Waffen-SS, we represented the political and military overlapping of PanEuropa. Among SS comrades were brothers in combat, ideological brothers. Our culture offered glory and social justice that we had never before seen. To the popular communities that composed Europe, we offered to overcome the concept of Nation by a higher concept, a Europe united in the harmony of popular communities. We were convinced that all Europeans would have recognized a federation rather than a domination in a *Bund*. We were convinced that in the measure in which we were strong militarily, strong enough to impose the supreme sacrifice, that we would have been able to impose our point of view on the populace."

Leibstandarte Adolf Hitler tanks and soldiers on a Milan street, September 1943. *Bussano*

October 1943

"Piazza San Sepolcro, Milan. Headquarters of the Fascist Federation of the Combat Fasces. On the first floor, coming in from Intra, where I joined the local Fascist Republican Party Federation, I ran into a meeting of Fascists in black shirts, about twenty around a conference table. There were no security measures for entrance into the building; anyone could enter. Among these was Diego Vassalli, class of 1899, who fought on the Carso, made the March on Rome, and enrolled in the Fascist Party in 1920, as well as having fought in Albania and the Greek-Albanian campaign as an officer in the 'M' battalions. There is a lot of loud shouting and a lot of confusion. Spirits are running high. Everyone expresses his own opinion; there are many 'ideas of revenge.' Then someone tries to calm down the most agitated. Talk begins about a 'State in Being' and its position in internal public law and in international law. The statutory reality of the RSI, a stability bought at a high price, because shadowy spirits were leaning toward a 'double cross.' Of the most complex sophism, victims of moral anemia that, unfortunately, military defeat had aggravated. Before the Italians lies a panorama of decadence of custom and spirit, which it would be pointless to ignore or minimize.

Leibstandarte Adolf Hitler tanks and soldiers in Piazza Duomo, Milan, September 1943. *Bussano*

"There is talk of political, socioeconomic custom, legal custom, everything, moreover investing morale, which has no objectivization. Even if individuals disagree about what to do, they all agreed about one thing: to arrest the traitors of the Grand Council and execute them for high treason. The 25th of July marked the breakup of Italian spiritual unity, and, as a consequence, it guaranteed the early Marxist revival that would characterize the phenomenon of separation and transfer of our national territory to foreigners, but also, it established the vanguard of the modern communist 'intelligentsia team.' I stayed there to listen to the yelling of those assembled there. Then I finally got tired and left. The building was empty, devoid of all furniture; my footsteps echoed as I went down the stairs, where there were no security measures. I went to Piazza Duomo; I wanted to take the streetcar home, then I changed my mind. I began to walk home. While I was walking, I thought about 'Fascism' and was convinced that philosophical theories were too weak to unite a people like the Italians. Fascism's most virulent enemy was the bourgeoisie. The bourgeoisie had always been indifferent to the working class and its political problems. I think of the Italian populace, after the hosannas of Fascism, and now I hate it."

Giuseppe Vassalli in civilian clothes

Legione SS Italiana

Giovani d'Italia! Voi siete gli eredi di quel patrimonio spirituale di grandezza e di libertà che va gelosamente custodito e difeso a tutti i costi, per l'avvenire della generazione futura.

Vorrete voi disperdere il frutto di tutti i sacrifici eroici compiuti dai vostri padri?

No! Voi siete italiani! Voi dunque dovete avere un sentimento di orgoglio nazionale e di onore! Scuotetevi! Liberatevi dal veleno del disfattismo e del pessimismo propinati dalla subdola propaganda nemica!

Giovani italiani, arruolatevi! Abbiate fede e ritroverete in Voi stessi l'innato indomito coraggio e l'amore patriottico della nostra razza!

La LEGIONE SS ITALIANA Vi attende!

La Legione SS Italiana accoglie i cittadini incondizionatamente idonei delle classi dal 1907 al 1927 comprese.

CENTRO DI ARRUOLAMENTO

MILANO - Via Maestri 2 (ang. Viale B. Maria), Tel. 50-147

Recruitment poster for the Italian SS Legion

Allied troops and equipment landing at Anzio, 1944

Panther tank and assault guns on the Anzio front, 1944

Joining the Waffen-SS

"In early February 1944, I join the National Socialist Party and am issued card number 2.191.367. My year group was recalled; I am able to enlist in the Waffen-SS. I go to Via Pietro Maestri 2 in Milan, headquarters of the Waffen-SS recruitment office. Sergeant Leopoldo Andreis greets me and introduces me to the boss, Major Giuseppe Cotta Ramusino. Ramusino questions me for about an hour as to why I have chosen the Waffen-SS. I reply with abundant cultural reasons to Major Ramusino's questions, and he finally enlists me conditionally. I have to get a medical exam at the Red Cross in Porta Venezia. I go to the Red Cross, where a doctor and a nurse receive me; the doctor examines me, the usual military medical exam. Then he gives me the document that states that I am fit as an enlistee. I report to the barracks in Via Suzzani."

Employment at the Front: Kampfgruppe Diebitsch

"After midnight on January 22, 1944, a massive Allied naval force, consisting of 133 warships and 241 transport and landing vessels, in addition to smaller craft, reached the shores off Anzio along the Pontine littoral. After a few minutes, the first landing craft, full of men and vehicles, made for the coast and reached it in three different points, at Anzio itself and to the north and south of that small city. Operation Shingle had begun, which according to the Anglo-American plans was aimed at flanking the Gustav Line and allowing for the rapid fall of Rome and the entire German front in Italy. The first German units sent by Feldmarschall Kesselring to oppose the landings were of course those that were available as reserves, in particular elements of the 4.Fallschirmjäger-Division, stationed in Perugia, and of Fallschirm-Panzer-Division Hermann Göring, stationed in Piverno, so that by the evening of January 22, forces totaling five battalions were in contact with the enemy forces that had landed, without however establishing a defensive front. Among the units upon which Kesselring's headquarters' attention was focused was the 16.SS-Pz.Gr.Div. RFSS, a newly formed division that was still being outfitted, with various units in training scattered all over central and northern Italy. The core of the division consisted of the SS-Sturmbrigade Reichsführer SS, which was engaged in Corsica."

Italian Troops on the Anzio Front

"A first unit of paratroopers arrived on the line on February 12, 1944. It was a reduced-strength battalion of about three hundred men, which dug in along the northern perimeter of the front along the line of Fosso della Moletta, integrated into the 4. Fallschirmjäger-Division. It was along with that division that the battalion was able to take part in the February 16 German counteroffensive, Operation Fischfang, during which, distinguishing itself in Allied eyes because of its fighting qualities and level of training, it was literally decimated, losing about half its men. A second Italian unit reached the operational area on March 3, 1944.

"This was the Barbarigo naval infantry battalion of the X MAS Division, which deployed in the southern part of the front, in the sector of the 715.Infanterie-Division. Its 1st Company was positioned in the Kampfgruppe Knöchlein sector of the line, where it remained until March 29, 1944, when it was

Italian paratroopers from the Nembo Battalion and German Fallschirmjäger Division on the Anzio front, 1944

relieved by legionnaires of 2.Kp. of the II./1. The operational employment of Italian SS troops was delayed because of problems with organizing and equipping the first battalion scheduled to be assigned to the front. Finally, in mid-February, SS-Ogruf. Wolff, who as commander in chief of the Italian volunteer legion was responsible for their operational employment, ordered the Kommandostab der italienischen Freiwilligen Legionen to ready a battalion of the newly constituted 1.Sturmbrigade for immediate deployment to the southern front. The German counteroffensive had been launched, which was supposed to smash the Allied bridgehead at Anzio. The battalion, officially the II.Bataillon / Infanterie-Regiment 1, was under the orders of Obersturmführer Carlo Federigo degli Oddi, who cut a fine figure as an old and experienced soldier. Born in Alexandria, Egypt, in the late 1800s, he came from an old and noble family from Siena, which had in its custody the standard of the ancient Republic of Siena, and a fragment of that standard had been sewn into the banner of the 97th Blackshirt Battalion and later into the combat flag of the II./1. A veteran of the First World War, he had participated in the pacification campaign in Libya, where he had spent many years in service with the Libyan permanent legions and in the campaign in East Africa. In February 1941, he assumed command of the 97th Blackshirt Battalion, with which he operated in Bosnia, Croatia, and Dalmatia until September 1943, when he joined the Germans with his entire unit, integrated into the Miliz Regiment De Maria. The battalion, designated the 1Bataillon italienische Freiwillige [of] Waffen-SS or 1.Bataillon Italia, also known as the 'Degli Oddi' Battalion, was structured with three companies and a headquarters company. Along with the other two battalions of Infanterie-Regiment 1 of 1.Sturmbrigade, it was to have constituted a *Kampfgruppe* of regimental strength under the orders of SS-Oberführer Karl Diebitsch. Because of the heavy losses to the 'Degli Oddi' Battalion, however, III./Inf.Rgt.1 was used to provide some of its personnel to II./Inf.Rgt.1, while 1.SS-Bataillon Debica was employed until the end of May 1944 in antipartisan operations in central Italy rather than on the Anzio front. We don't know why. For this writer, the Debica was the best battalion in the division, the best among 20,000 men. This led to a situation in which Kampfgruppe Diebitsch consisted in practice of only II./Inf.Rgt.1, other than for a support unit and a field hospital.

Marines of the Barbarigo on the Anzio front, March 1944

Soldiers of the Fallschirm-Panzer-Division Hermann Göring at the Anzio front passing by a damaged Elefant tank destroyer

German soldiers in a cane field in the Anzio-Nettuno bridgehead, 1944

Carlo Federigo degli Oddi

German defensive position at Anzio, 1944

"The structure of the support unit consisted of a food and ammunition depot and a propaganda detachment under Ostuf. Raimondo Cisari, which had several war correspondents, the most notable of whom was Oscha. Alessandro Nicolini, who came from the GNR officer cadet school of Fontanellato and was the author of many articles for the legion's weekly newspaper, *Avanguardia*. The field hospital was managed by Hstuf. Doctor Tullio Bracco. Strength of the three companies was about 120 each, structured with three rifle platoons, each with an officer and some thirty NCOs and soldiers, and a machine gun platoon with an officer and about twenty NCOs and soldiers and equipped with four Breda Mod. 37 heavy machine guns. The battalion also had ten 81 mm mortars. Subordinate to the Stabs-Kompanie was a mortar platoon led by an officer, equipped with six tubes, while the other four mortars were issued to the rifle companies. The armament was exclusively Italian, but with a greater number of Beretta submachine guns than was normal in Regio Esercito battalions. The only shortcoming of consequence was the complete lack of antitank weapons, which was remedied when the battalion was already on the line either by training the troops to use the *Panzerfaust* as well as sending a battery of German 75 mm Pak 40 antitank guns with Italian crews from Pinerolo, drawn from the Sturmbrigade antitank group. All told, the 650 volunteers were armed with 421 Mod. 91/38 carbines, 131 Beretta MAB submachine guns, 130 Beretta pistols, fifty Breda 30 light machine guns, twelve Breda 27 heavy machine guns, and ten 81 mm mortars. At the time of departure from Milan on March 13, 1944, II./Inf.Rgt.1 had thirty-two officers, ninety-three NCOs, and 525 other ranks. The high number of officers and NCOs compared to the number of troops is explained by the fact that efforts were made to make up for the lack of training by increasing the number of corporals, who, by their nature, were more capable and reliable than were private soldiers.

"The personnel were in fact drawn from the various specialties of the Regio Esercito and thus had a certain level of training, combat experience, and extremely varied motivations behind them. Alongside the Blackshirts were bersaglieri, alpine troopers, and ordinary drivers; veterans of the various campaigns in

An Italian SS Legion rifle squad armed with 91/38 carbines, taken during an exercise. *Corbatti*

Africa and Russia worked alongside young volunteers who had only a few months' service under their belts. The limited time available prevented development of an integrated team and generalized combat training according to Waffen-SS criteria. A lot was thus left to combat experience and the technical preparation of the veterans, especially of the officers and NCOs. The battalion's prolonged stay in Milan did not undermine the unit's high degree of morale, as the regimental headquarters had feared, worried about possible negative influences deriving from contact with civilians. To the contrary, many young men reported as volunteers to the barracks on Via Suzzani, some of whom were indeed enlisted.

"The atmosphere that surrounded II./Inf.Rgt. at that time was exciting and enthusiastic. On March 12, 1944, at the battalion's headquarters, Generalleutnant Canevari addressed the officers of II./Inf.Rgt.1 as follows: 'Fellow officers, not one step back! You are not going to cut a fancy figure, but only to die! Your behavior will determine whether or not the Germans rearm an Italian army.'"

A German assault gun at the Anzio front, March 1944

On the Anzio Front

"The battalion left Milan by train at 0700 on March 13, 1944, from the Greco station, headed for Littoria. At the moment of departure, twenty-two workers boarded the train, most of whom were Communists from the nearby Pirelli works at Biocca, who accompanied the legionnaires for most of the trip and were kept under the watchful eyes of the officers. The long and slow journey along an Italian railway system that was partially destroyed by bombings lasted almost a week. The trip

Soldiers and a Tiger tank at the Anzio bridgehead, March 1944

German soldiers on the road between Anzio and Nettuno, March 1944

German tanks and soldiers in the Anzio-Nettuno bridgehead

A crossroads in the combat zone. *BA*

allowed the legionnaires to show themselves in the streets of various towns, giving rise to amazement among the populace, which was no longer accustomed to seeing Italian soldiers bearing weapons. The battalion made it to south of Rome by train, then continued on to the front by truck, arriving during the night between March 19 and 20, 1944. Kampfgruppe Diebitsch, of which II./1 was supposed to have been the lead element, was assigned to LXXVI.Pz.Korps and subordinated to 715.Inf.Div. (led by Generalleutnant Hans-Georg Hildebrandt). The Italian volunteers were integrated into the defensive positions held by the two *Kampfgruppen* of 16.SS-Pz. Gr.Div. RFSS. The first unit to reach the line on March 21, was 1.Kompanie, under Ustuf. Buldrini, deployed in the II./SS-Pz.Gr.Rgt.35 (Kampfgruppe Dieterichs) sector, while 2. and 3.Kp. entered the line on March 22; this writer was part of 2.Kompanie, in the sector held by II./SS-Pz.Gr.Rgt.36 (Kampfgruppe Knöchlein). Troops from 2.Kompanie relieved the 1st Company of the Barbarigo Battalion, dug in along the banks of the Mussolini Canal, whose ranks were very depleted after losses sustained in little more than two weeks on the front line. During February the Germans had launched a series of strong offensives to wipe out the bridgehead that focused on the front facing and north of Cisterna, while to the south of that town there were secondary actions, so that the two opposing armies had allotted only a thin screen of troops to occupy that area. The Anglo-American side had concentrated the bulk of their forces in the eastern and northeastern sectors of the front, between Cisterna and Aprilia, key points in their defensive system. Farther south, about 13 kilometers [8 mi.] from the sea (Torre Astura) at bridge number 5 on the Mussolini Canal, near the town of Sessano, or about a quarter of the perimeter of the entire bridgehead, positions were held by the First Special Service Force, a mixed US-Canadian elite force, with a strength of little more than 1,200 men. The next stretch of the front was held by another elite unit, the 504th Parachute Infantry Regiment of the US 82nd Airborne Division, known to the Italian SS volunteers as the 'Kansas City Division.' The Germans as well, who were concerned about concentrating the major part of their forces for the massive February offensives between the Moletta Canal to the north and Cisterna and Isola Bella to the east, had neglected the southern part of the front and, in the haste in which they had amassed as many troops as possible to slow down and then halt the Allied advance inland in the days immediately following the landings, had focused their attention to safeguarding unit integrity and avoid damaging comingling in the areas slated for the planned offensives.

"To cover the stretches of the front considered secondary, such as that south of Cisterna, headquarters of 14.Armee did not hesitate to employ the most-varied units, gathered since the second half of February, subordinate to 715.Inf.Div., which in turn was part of LXXVI.Pz.Korps. Alongside the soldiers of that division and the *SS Kampfgruppen*, from time to time there were battalions of the Fallschirm-Pz.Div. HG, the LW.Jg.Btl.7, the Barbarigo battalion of the Decima MAS, several

An Elefant tank destroyer of s.Pz.Jg.Abt.653 and Panthers at the Anzio front

A German corporal, March 1944

companies of the ROA, the Russian liberation army, consisting of former Red Army prisoners of war enlisted in the Wehrmacht, and various other minor German units, among which was a *Nebelwerfer* rocket launcher battalion and, in May, the 3.Kp./s. Pz.Abt.508, which was an independent battalion equipped with Tiger heavy tanks. It should not then be surprising that the German headquarters would send the newly arrived II./1 to that sector of the front, considered quiet and thus ideal for the baptism of fire of the unit, which had been prepared in such haste and for which there was no guarantee that it could hold under stressful combat conditions. Along with these objective considerations of the situation, German prejudice with respect to newly formed Italian units, which were considered unreliable and thus to be employed with due caution in quiet areas of the front and parceled out as much as possible among German units, probably also played a role. The unchallenged superiority of enemy ground and naval artillery and complete Anglo-American air superiority, along with the almost complete lack of obstacles to observation, made any type of movement during daylight practically impossible, often forcing the Italian volunteers to keep their legs immersed in water and mud up to their calves in order to have a minimum amount of cover in the shallow individual foxholes, which could be dug only with the utmost difficulty, since water began to surface after digging down only about 50 or 60 centimeters [1.6–2.0 ft.]. After the initial Allied offensive, which was contained by German troops who then went on the counterattack on February 16 and almost managed to throw the invasion force back into the sea, the front had stabilized and the combat devolved into a wearying war of position, of raids and clashes between patrols in no-man's land.

"Following an initial period of adjustment, spent mainly in consolidating the defensive system, the Italian volunteers began a period of intense patrol activity, both to familiarize themselves with enemy positions as well as to try to take prisoners, in addition to carrying out raids to wipe out or occupy particularly

Fallschirmjäger with a mortar on the Anzio front, March 1944

dangerous or threatening enemy positions. This was the main activity carried out by the legionnaires of II./1 during their time at the Anzio front, an activity that was as gloomy as it was hard and necessary. The Germans, and with them Italian soldiers, had to deal with Allied air dominance, which was challenged only by flak, and with the heavy Allied naval fire, whose range enabled it to hit almost any part of the German front. Paralyzed during the day, activity on the front resumed at night with construction projects and burrowing in the front lines, stringing barbed wire, and laying mines, as well as patrol actions. There were many losses during this dangerous and nerve-wracking activity, often caused by enemy minefields. The II./1 went into combat completely devoid of any antitank capability.

German paratrooper in a defensive position

Fallschirmjäger moving in the mud and water, 1944

Carroceto sector, a Grille SP gun moving amid the ruins of a small town. In the background are a Sherman and a German half-track, abandoned by their crews.

The Aprilia area under Allied bombardment, March 1944

"The Italian volunteers were hurriedly trained in the use of the *Panzerfaust* by their German comrades. That weapon, truly deadly at close range against tanks as well as in destruction of fixed enemy positions, turned out to be indispensable to fill the gap in the Italian arsenal in the field of short-range combat against tanks, replacing individual attacks against tanks by using mines and Molotov cocktails. Until the beginning of the American offensive, patrol actions were the main activity carried out by the battalion. These were actions that wore one down and were depressing, tiring, weakening the men . . . but morale of the Italian SS volunteers always remained high, stimulated by the example of their German comrades.

"During the nights of April 16 and 17, the two German *SS Kampfgruppen* were gradually retired from the line and sent to their original stations in order to complete the formation of the 16.SS-Pz.Gren.Div RFSS. Their places were taken by Infanterie-Regiment 1028 of 715.Inf. Div., commanded by Oberst Mangold.

"During the night of May 11–12, Operation Diadem began: the US 5th Army and the British 8th Army began their attack against Montecassino and the Gustav Line in order to break through and, in concert with an attack against the bridgehead at Anzio, to surround and destroy the German 10.Armee and then occupy Rome. The Italian Waffen-SS were right in the middle of the enemy attack and, after fierce resistance, were overrun; overall losses were almost 70 percent of the battalion's strength."

Operation Hochland: The Ghemme Hills, Piedmont, February 1945

"My II./82 took part in Operation Hochland;[2] the sweep began in February 1945 in Valsesia (Piedmont). On February 12, 1945,[3] a unit of ours, consisting of a rifle platoon and one of Breda 37 machine guns—as carried by this writer, and the tripod [was carried] by Sergio Failoni and the first ammo case by De Manzolin, who was an Istrian from Parenzo, a Fascist who was categorically opposed to national socialism—marched along a path that cut a vineyard in two. We went forward cautiously, since this was the territory of Cino Moscatelli.[4] Halfway there we came under attack: strong rifle fire announced the attack; it was the 84th Brigade Strisciante Musati[5] that was attacking us. Our commanding officer blew a whistle, ordering us to assume defensive positions. We quickly went down the slopes of the vineyard and deployed for combat. Our formation assumed a 'V' formation with the Breda 37 at its base. The partisans, seeing us pull back, thought that they had scattered us, but it was a tactic that we had practiced many times during training. No losses on the first move. The partisans fired without any preestablished plan, which generally is the concept of fire discipline. There was no tactic to deal with the range of fire of the machine guns. Their instinct was to fire and keep on firing, because they could not find the proper targets.

"Their concept of fire discipline should have been better; the partisan machine guns did not have a sufficient arc of fire. For thirty minutes the partisans tried to advance, but then they quit. They are trapped in the 'V'; their fire becomes weaker. Partisan losses are high; we lose no one, not even a scratch. Facing us are the armed representatives of communism; they are not trained, and it is apparent. They are full of the will to fight, but it was an unrealistic attack. The tops of the 'V' close in; we see groups of partisans running up the hill. Our soldiers are given a sharp order: 'Fix bayonets!' It's hand to hand. He who is better trained will win. At the first whistle, the comrades come out into the open and aim at the enemy. Fifteen minutes of fierce fighting, and the surviving partisans raise their hands. They are very elegant; they have brown uniforms—red tabs with Bolshevik insignia. They are morally defeated. They had attacked us, numerically superior, convinced that they would beat us in battle because of the greater size of their unit, a ratio of three to one. The prisoners are searched; we find propaganda leaflets edited by Palmiro Togliatti, personal documents that we return to them, weapons. The battle is over; the ramshackle 84th Brigade Strisciante Musati has been destroyed by a few men of the Italian SS. Destroyed and humiliated.

"In the book *Il Monterosa è sceso a Milano*, written by Paolo Secchia and Cino Moscatelli, the episode cited by me, as are many other episodes, is forgotten. For political reasons the Strisciante Musati was given secondary mention, given its heavy and humiliating defeat. It is at this point that the tenor voice of one of our comrades sings a song dear to us: 'Anely, you are the child of my heart; I gave my first love only to you; I will come.' The whole unit sings Anely; it is a song of liberation, syrupy sweet and liberating. We fought against Communist partisans . . . among the prisoners were many women. At night, there are interrogations. One partisan behaved with dignified courage, declared himself a convinced Communist, and underwent the interrogation calmly. I asked the officer in charge if I could ask

German soldier armed with a *Panzerfaust*

Allied tank and motorized forces on the march, 1944

SS volunteers training at Rodengo-Saiano. *AC*

The II./82 drawn up at the end of an exercise at Rodengo-Saiano. In the foreground is Ostubaf. Giorleo. *Corbatti*

Italian SS volunteers armed with Breda machine guns and MAB submachine guns

A detachment of Italian SS volunteers in an open field. *Corbatti*

the prisoner a few questions: 'How could a Communist like you let himself be captured?' His face darkened: 'During the assault, a grenade exploded near me, I lost consciousness. I imagine that my buddies left me for dead. When I came to, I was in your hands. There was nothing I could do about it,' he said sadly."

Mortirolo: The Final Battle

Laying down arms at Fondo, May 5, 1945

"In early April 1945, the Waffen-SS battalion[6] stationed at Ceremate (Como) set out for Val Camonica in open trucks. From Lake d'Iseo we arrived at Darfo. From Darfo we drove along the Oglio River to Edolo. In Edolo, the battalion sent out units to Trivigno, Suspessa, Vezza d'Oglio, and Temù. A rifle company and two machine gun platoons set off on foot to the Mortirolo and dug in at Biorca. A sweep called Azione Mughetto is under way; participating along with the Italian Waffen-SS are the I and LXIII Battalions of the Tagliamento Blackshirt Assault Legion and two companies of the 5th Mobile Black Brigade Quagliata (alpine) on the Mortirolo, 1,066 meters [3,496 ft.] above Edolo. It is the final attempt to conquer the Mortirolo. From Biorca, combat against the partisan formation begins; it is the final push against the partisans led by British officers. We, the Waffen-SS, were housed in small huts, against which the partisans were firing with 81 mm mortars and machine guns. I have to say that their aim was good, much better than Ciro Moscatelli's Garibaldini. While I was on guard behind a window, a burst grazed the wooden frame on the left. On another occasion, again with a machine gun, while I was getting out of a foxhole where we had set up our Breda 37, while going into a hut a burst hit the entrance stairway dead center.

A group of partisans captured in a sweep, February 1945

SS volunteers. *Corbatti*

"Second Lieutenant Bianchi helped me emplace the Breda 37 on a pyramidal pile of manure. It's only me and the officer; my assistant gunner is wounded. Lieutenant Bianchi offers to be my assistant, I load the Breda, and while I am firing, Bianchi begins to recite Goethe's 'Prometheus': 'Here I stay; I create men in my image and likeness, a race that suffers and cries, and how I have contempt for you, Jove.' Three prisoners were captured during another hand-to-hand engagement, one of whom was wounded. During the withdrawal, the prisoner was taken to Valle on our unit's stretcher. Between April 26 and 28, excited partisan voices announced Mussolini's death to us. We of the Waffen-SS had always been on the attack. The shock we felt upon hearing of Mussolini's death was heavy, and everyone in our unit is now aware of the inescapable end of the conflict in which we were engaged. On April 28, when the order to withdraw was given, a surreal silence fell over Valle. The Italian Waffen-SS began their retreat with their comrades from the Tagliamento and the Quagliata Black Brigade.

Giuseppe Vassalli, *first on the left*, with other soldiers from his unit during a training exercise. *Saronno*

"We marched in two files along the unpaved road. It took us two days to get to the bottom of the valley. The partisans did not attack us, partly because they had abandoned their fortified and advantageous positions and would have had to fight us in the open. On the floor of the valley, the units no longer with orders clogged the road that led from the Tonale Pass. Tagliamento, Black Brigades, Italian Waffen-SS, Germans. At Ponte di Legno, we part ways with our German comrades.

"The episode: A truck column with sand-colored 'M' insignia was carrying German troops in camouflage uniforms and armed with small arms. The trucks had been abandoned by the Tagliamento to the south, out of gas. The 'M' legionnaires then claimed the trucks;

Partisans captured during a sweep and searched by German soldiers

SS volunteer with submachine gun

upon clear refusal by the Germans, an 'M' legionnaire, with a P38 in his hand, went behind the first truck in the column and began to shoot at the tires. I leave it to the imagination of the reader to picture the expression on the faces of the German soldiers, among them a youngster with carrot-colored hair and with eyes wide open and incredulous. On May 1, at the Tonale Pass, my unit stayed at the DUX barracks, where we slept on three-tiered bunk beds. There was a snowstorm outside. On the road to the north we found a Feldgendarmerie truck that had fallen into a stream. A team of firemen from Trento Province were recovering the bodies, using ropes. The corpses that were resting with their chests on the ground emitted a macabre death rattle because of the air and water that had accumulated. The leader of the firemen's team, wearing a liberty helmet, asked us if we wanted to contribute some money for the work they did. Upon seeing our looks of amazement, he said, 'Right, you have other things to think about.' The transfer march from Tonale to Fondo was not a transfer, but the march of an army in retreat. The retreat was complex and difficult and at times dramatic. The column was very long, kilometers of combatants, tired, wounded in their pride, without any leadership. My Waffen-SS unit acted as a rear guard; many of us, the most physically fit, in addition to the normal guard duties, volunteered for patrols so that we would not be surprised by the enemy. And then the thing that no one remembers: the hunger! With an empty stomach for days, no prophet's beard can make an armed unit move at a normal pace. Our boots were treading on territory of the Italian Social Republic. For this writer, they were days of an ethical and moral intensity that have no equal. On May 5, 1945, the Waffen-SS unit reached Fondo in Val di Sole (Trento). We found out that American tanks had surrounded us. We decide to turn our weapons in to the local Carbinieri station. We didn't surrender to anyone! I turn in my Breda 37 and give my name, surname, and serial number to the sergeant in charge. My issue pistol and fighting dagger I bury under an oak tree at the local orphanage and would return many years later to reclaim them. We were misguided soldiers because we fought a desperate war and knew it was lost, all the while trying to be faithful to our oath. Maybe we were misguided because we were fascinated by a myth that was not human, convinced that we belonged to a warrior order of supermen; we paid with enormous losses in a bloodbath, the myth in which we believed, a new Europe."

Machine gun squad of Uscha. Siniero of the II./82. *Foreground, from the left*, Sturmmann Boldi and SS Legionnaire Giuseppe Vassalli. *Corbatti*

One of the last photos of Mussolini, April 1945

II./82 machine gun platoon on the march. *Corbatti*

Two NCOs of II./82. *On the left*, Scharführer Gargiulo, with the three-arrow insignia, and Unterscharführer Luigi Burbbi. Gargiulo was killed in late April at Mortirolo. *Corbatti*

One of the last photos of Giuseppe Vassalli, at a ceremony commemorating the dead of the Italian Social Republic. *Corbatti*

SS legionnaires of the II./82 on the march. *Corbatti*

Alessandro Scano, *first on the right*, legionnaire in the Tagliamento. *Scano*

Chapter XIII
ALESSANDRO SCANO: FROM THE TAGLIAMENTO TO THE WAFFEN-SS

Scano (*indicated by the arrow*) at Massa in 1943

Lieutenant Davide Scano, prior to September 8, 1943

Soldiers of the Guardia Nazionale Repubblicana

Alessandro Scano was born on January 25, 1927, in Turin. His military career began in May 1943, when after having been able to get his parents to consent, he enlisted in the Regia Marina and was assigned to the navy school at Forte dei Marmi. He signed up to take a radioman's course and was selected for submarine duty. However, before he could be posted, the events of September 8 happened and all was in total confusion, and the officers at the school left the students to deal with the events themselves. Young Alessandro then took a train to Turin and from there went to Chieri, where his family had moved. His father, Davide, an officer in the Regio Esercito, had been captured in France by the Germans but was among the first to join the new Italian Social Republic.

Alessandro also decided to join the forces of the new Italian Social Republic, reporting to the Damorbida barracks in Turin, where the early recruits for the GNR, the Guardia Nazionale Repubblicana[1] (Republican National Guard), were assembled. Although only sixteen years old, he was given a uniform and put to work guarding the door of the barracks. Along with him were about ten other young volunteers, who at the time constituted the only armed Fascist force in Turin. Two weeks of never-ending guard duty and patrols followed, especially at night. With the arrival of new recruits, a first company was formed that was sent to Rivoli for a period of training under the orders of Lieutenant Sergio Schianici. During this relatively quiet period, there were only occasional clashes with the partisans, who limited themselves to making attacks at night against our sentinels, firing from a notable distance, which in most cases never wounded anyone. Only on one occasion did thing go differently, as Scano himself relates: "One night a roadblock on a secondary road was attacked in a more determined manner. Our position consisted of three soldiers with a Breda 30 light machine gun; a good friend of mine named Seves was the gunner. He was hit by a burst of fire, and although four rounds hit him in the torso, luckily none of them hit any vital organs and he returned fire, causing the attackers to flee. He fainted on his weapon because of the loss of so much blood. That guy, a giant over 6 feet tall, healed quickly, so much so that he was on his feet again after about ten days."

With the Tagliamento

In early 1944, Scano's company was transferred to Vercelli, where it joined up with the men of the new Tagliamento Legion. The 63rd CCNN Assault Legion Tagliamento, after having been on the Eastern Front until 1943, was returned to Italy following the second defensive battle of the Don. The legion consisted of the LXIII CCNN Battalion Udine and the LXXIX CCNN Battalion Reggio Emilia. Very few veterans returned from the terrible battles on the Russian front. After September 8, 1943, even before the birth of the RSI, the LXIII Battalion was commanded by Colonel Merico Zuccari, determined not to lay down his arms and to continue to fight alongside his German ally. Along with other units, he thus became part of 2. Fallschirmjäger-Division. With the establishment of the Italian Social Republic, the unit was designated the 1st Assault Division "M" Tagliamento, integrated into the Republican National Guard, remaining under command of Colonel Zuccari. The Tagliamento was initially employed in the Apennine Mountains in sweep operations searching for Anglo-American prisoners who had escaped from prison camps. In late November, it was moved to the province of Brescia and on December 19, 1943, to the Vercelli area, where it remained until spring of 1944. Its headquarters was set up in the Conte barracks in Turin, which the legionnaires quickly renamed Tagliamento barracks. Scano's company was assigned to the LXIII Battalion, commanded by Captain Alimonia. At Vercelli, Scano was promoted to corporal: "I commanded a platoon, but I never gave up my Breda 30 machine gun, for which I had been team chief until that time. The Breda 30 was a weapon with many faults; it jammed easily and had a short effective range. We carried it slung from the shoulder, like a submachine gun, and we often fired it from the hip, steadying it with the bipod."[2] After several weeks of intensive training, the unit was sent to Val Sesia to flush out a Communist partisan band led by Vincenzo Moscatelli, also known as Cino,[3] who controlled all the partisan forces in the Vercelli and Biella areas. The company set up its operational base at Rimasco, a small town a few kilometers from the Swiss border; from there, every morning the legionnaires left to conduct sweeps: "Our approach tactic to the zone where there was presumed partisan activity was to get as close as possible by truck, then to proceed on foot. If the terrain was open, we advanced in open formation, spread out several meters from each other so as to offer the smallest target possible, while two or three patrols were sent out ahead. When the lay of the land did not allow this maneuver (mule tracks, steep and narrow mountain trails), we went in single file with a good distance between each other. Our personal armament consisted of the Beretta SMG, dagger, and Breda 30 light machine gun (which was my issue weapon), while the unit also had Breda 37 machine guns and 81 mm mortars. Pistols were not issued, although almost everyone had one.

Scano (*indicated by the arrow*) at the Rivoli barracks after September 8, 1943. Note the Breda 30 and the gunners' accoutrements.

GNR legionnaires and German soldiers of the Polizei during a sweep in Piedmont, spring 1944. *Corbatti*

Mussolini inspecting a group of Tagliamento legionnaires

A Tagliamento legionnaire

Italian SS officers: *center*, Colonel Degli Oddi; *on the left*, Lieutenant Davide Scano

"I swapped my Beretta 7.65 pistol, taken from a partisan and much sought by the Germans, with a German messenger's P.38; in addition to being an excellent weapon, it had the advantage of using a 9 mm round, the same as that of the submachine gun, so there was always plenty of ammunition. Other units had 47 mm antitank and 20 mm antiaircraft guns; obviously these heavy weapons were not suited for sweep operations in the mountains that our unit carried out. As a final note, the other RSI units wore the Gladio, not the red 'M.'"[4]

Transfer to the Waffen-SS

After having been wounded during a sweep in Val Sesia, Scano returned home for a period of rest. Here he finally saw his father[5] again, who had also been wounded on the Nettuno front with the Degli Oddi Battalion and had been awarded the Iron Cross Second Class. This encounter convinced him to transfer to the Italian SS, in the same Degli Oddi Battalion. The uniform remained that of the GNR, on which he put the insignia reserved for the Italian SS units that had fought on the front lines. Individual armament was similar to that issued to the Tagliamento: only some of the unit equipment was different, with the issue of several MG42 machine guns in addition to the Breda 30 and Breda 37 machine guns. The SS battalion was garrisoned in Pinerolo, in Turin Province, in the Pinerolo cavalry barracks. Sweep operations followed in the Bergamo area, with bases at Lake d'Iseo and Sestriere in the Pinerolo area. The unit was then sent to the Como area, at Mariano Comense, where it remained until the end of the war. Let us look at Scano's direct testimony:[6] "Relations with our comrades had always been marked by the greatest friendship, with the Germans as well, even though at times we could sense, understandably given the precedent, a vague sense of aloofness. With respect to our superiors, there was a marked difference between the Italians and the Germans. With the Italian officers there had always been, both in the Tagliamento and in the SS, a respectful but cordial relationship, and in some cases also of friendship, this being certainly due to all of the volunteers being animated by common sentiments. The German officers, on the other hand, were mainly of high

Italian SS Legion soldiers, with camouflage uniforms, during an antipartisan operation. *Corbatti*

social standing, almost a privileged class of German society. For us there was, at least at that time, discipline, but an outlook on life that I would say understood that circumstances were not normal, but the Germans were fair but very rigid."

Following the move to Mariano Comense, a relatively quiet period began for Scano's unit. The Italian volunteers were engaged in normal administrative tasks, manning roadblocks and almost never in real operations against partisan bands. Let us look again at Scano:[7] "Despite the fact that in Feldgendarmerie service, a service that we carried out in pairs, we were extremely vulnerable and visible, we wore a gorget on our chest with the inscription 'Feldgendarmerie' [and] we never had the slightest problem. This apparent calm (everything would explode a few months later) debunks the rhetoric that was always touted by the resistance; that is, that during the final months of the war the partisans were in complete control of the territory. Nothing is further from the truth." In the autumn of 1944, Scano's unit took part in a sweep in the Bergamo area. During a pause in the operation near a stream, Scano, who was tired and hot from marching, refreshed himself and drank copiously. Continuing the march alongside the stream, the corpses of two partisans in

Summer 1944, a mixed group of German, Italian SS, and GNR legionnaires getting ready for an action against the partisans. *Corbatti*

advanced state of putrefaction were spotted. Returning to the base, Scano began to feel sick and suffered from an increasingly high temperature. He was admitted to the hospital at Mariano, where he was diagnosed with a severe case of paratyphoid fever. He had drunk infected water.

While he was convalescing, Scano met Marshal Graziani, who had made a visit to the wounded to give awards to those most deserving. In early 1945, the Italian SS units in Brianza had a quiet time, maintaining good relations with the local citizens.

Italian SS legion soldiers wearing camouflage uniforms during an antipartisan operation. *Corbatti*

Marshal Rodolfo Graziani

Toward the End

During the night of April 24, all units in the Como region were put in a state of alarm. On board a truck, a group of about thirty men, Italians and Germans, made a sweep around several towns around Como, Erba, Asso, Canzo, and other towns. The situation had deteriorated, barracks had been abandoned by the soldiers, and chaos reigned everywhere. At dawn, the group tried to return to Mariano to rejoin the rest of the unit, but when they reached Vighizzolo, it was attacked by a partisan group along the road. Let us again see Scano's testimony:[8] "Passing through Vighizzolo, a town not far from Mariano, we were attacked by a group of partisans positioned on both sides of the road. There was a furious firefight, with a couple of men killed right away. . . . While we returned fire, we pulled back to a farmhouse that was in the middle of a large plot of land, open on all sides and thus easy to defend. Positioned in this house, we resisted repeated attempts by the partisans to break in. Seeing the good position that we were in, and it being extremely dangerous to approach us, three times a priest and a delegation of partisans, raising a white flag to call a ceasefire, tried to get us to surrender. The first two times we refused to surrender, hoping that a friendly unit might happen by and come to our rescue. The last time, the platoon leader, a young German paratroop lieutenant, asked the partisans for a few minutes to decide what to do. He got us together and said that he would like to refuse to surrender again, but considering that we were almost out of ammunition, he suggested that we surrender to avoid useless bloodshed. He charged one of us to let the partisans know that we accepted their proposal; he saluted us one last time and, without letting

German soldiers captured by partisans, late April 1945

German soldiers laying down their arms

us know what he was up to, went into another room. A few moments later we heard one last shot: he had taken his own life rather than be taken prisoner. . . . A few minutes later, having laid down our weapons and gone out into the open, we found ourselves facing a wall of infuriated humanity: peasants with hoes, pitchforks, and clubs, who tried to lynch us.

"In all honesty I have to say that it was the partisans themselves, in that moment, making a cordon around us, who saved us from a situation that was becoming desperate. We knew that it was certainly not due to any magnanimity toward us, since they had other plans. After a brief period, perhaps an hour, they brought us outside and lined us up against the wall, with the clear intent of resolving our problem in the way that suited them best; that is to say, by shooting us. On the other hand, the men drawn up in front of us, with their weapons in their hands, left no doubt about it. I had always thought that in life, everything is written in our own book of destiny, and in that page in my book the final word had not yet been written. In that instant, in fact, I heard the sound of engines, and a man came running, shouting, 'Run, run! The Germans are near!' The firing squad scattered; everyone sought refuge and, obviously, brought us with them. . . . They later brought us to a farmstead, where we were locked up in a hayloft. As night came, a guy came in who, with no wasted breath, told us that they would shoot us the next day. . . . In the early morning hours, when we awoke, we realized that the Germans who had been taken prisoner with us were no longer there. During the night, with hasty and silent negotiations, some German officers had reached an agreement to free their men. Resigned to my fate, I awaited events to unfold . . . I was going to die, with no sorrow, but with the only regret being not able to embrace my mother and father for one last time.

"Around midmorning, a man appeared at the door of the hayloft where we were being kept. . . . He approached me and asked me why we were there. . . . I answered that I would gladly have left, but that the partisans who were keeping us prisoner had already decreed that we were condemned to death. That man's response was 'As long as I am in command, no one gets killed here.' . . . The man took our names and cities of residence and left, saying, 'I'll send you home soon.' After a couple of hours, he returned with papers in his hand; they were our safe-conduct passes, and, after having given them to us and wishing us good luck, he let us go free."

German soldiers in Milan following the surrender, 1945

American tanks in Piazza del Duomo, Milan, April 1945

After having gotten civilian clothes, the soldiers headed for home. Scano, with another two friends, headed for Milan. Along the way he was captured by another group of partisans, again risking being shot. He miraculously escaped death, and, having gotten their safe-conduct passes back, the three managed to flee during the night. After wandering about, on May 1 Scano reached Turin, finding shelter in an aunt's home. About ten days later he learned of his father's death at the hands of the partisans. As Alessandro testifies, "He was arrested on April 25, 1945, at Mariano Comense by a band of independent partisans. Upon being pointed out by a cowardly traitor, a former soldier in the unit, he was identified along with two other officers, one of whom was Colonel Degli Oddi, and three civilians as being dangerous persons. Due to the intervention of a local civilian, who had guessed at the tragedy that was about to unfold, the parish priest of Mariano was called so that he could bring six consecrated hosts for communion for those to be executed. The priest tried to intercede with the partisans (who were not locals but had come from Milan), saying, 'Are you sure that these men are guilty? Let them at least be judged by a regular trial.' The answer was 'They have confessed to their guilt.' For the three military men, their guilt was represented by the uniform that they wore. The priest than asked for a stay of a quarter of an hour and sought out the mayor, whom he could not find. The priest quickly returned and found that five of the prisoners had already been executed; Colonel Degli Oddi was spared because it was felt that he could provide valuable information. Turning to the leader of those assassins, the priest said, 'And what if you killed innocent men?' The terse answer was 'We assume responsibility.' Thus was the life of Davide Scano, an Italian who had dedicated all of himself to his homeland, cut short."

Tiger I "Strolch" of schwere Panzerkompanie Meyer on the Italian front, assigned to s.Pz.Abt.508 in 1944

Chapter XIV
GIULIANO BORTOLOTTI: ITALIAN SS LEGION VOLUNTEER

Propaganda ad appearing in period newspapers urging enlistment in the Italian SS Legion

Giuliano Bortolotti wearing the Italian SS uniform. Note the black tabs with the double runes.

German tanks engaged at the Anzio bridgehead. *NA*

Giuliano Bortolotti, a native of Bologna born in 1925, joined the Italian Social Republic and was assigned to the Italian SS Legion. After the war, Giuliano wrote out his wartime memoirs in a very nice book, published in March 2007 by the Libreria Bottazzi.[1] In 1942, although still under age, he was able to enlist in the Milizia and, after completing his training, was assigned in the IX Legion, stationed on Pantellieria. On June 10, 1943, before the island surrendered to Anglo-American forces, young Bortolotti was transferred to Trapani to an 88 mm antiaircraft battery of the DICAT (Territorial Air Defense). Shortly before the Allied landings in Sicily, Bortolotti was sent to the mainland and then by train to the North. Sent like many other Italian soldiers to Germany after September 8, to the camp at Münsingen, he was among the earliest to choose to fight alongside the Germans, "for my country and for myself," as he later wrote.[2] On November 11, 1943, he swore an oath to Hitler and a few weeks later returned to Italy along with the 1st Armed Militia Regiment (Waffen Miliz), led by Waffen Sturmbannführer Paolo De Maria, with headquarters in Milan.

An Sd.Kfz.9 half-track towing a damaged Tiger I of 3./schw.Pz.Abt.508, March 1944

As happened with all the other personnel of the Waffen Miliz, the volunteers were issued varying types of uniform, all different, but with the red tabs: "It was said that we would get the black one only after having shown on the battlefield that we deserved them."[3] Bortolotti was assigned to the *SS-Stabskompanie* (headquarters company) of II Battalion of the 1st Regiment, commanded by Degli Oddi, as an orderly. On March 13, 1944, his unit left for the southern front, to be employed on the Nettunia front. The trip took five days because of Allied air attacks. After their having reached Orte on March 18, a German truck convoy carried the Italian legionnaires to the station at Littoria, where they spent the night. Anxious to get to the front line, Bortolotti managed to take the place of a legionnaire in the 3rd Platoon of 1.Kompanie, led by Waffen-Ustuf. Pio Filippani-Ronconi. The company was in turn subordinate to Waffen-Hauptsturmführer Remo Buldrini: "At Anzio-Nettuno, the Bataillon Degli Oddi was attached to Kampfgruppe Diebitsch, led by SS-Oberführer Karl Diebitsch, and prepared for trench warfare. We spent entire days in holes 60 to 70 centimeters [2.0–2.3 ft.] deep, created by shells from enemy naval gunfire. It was impossible to make them any safer, because if you began to dig, you soon ran into water since the Anglo-Americans had blown up the Mussolini Canal, transforming the area occupied by the Italo-German troops into an immense marsh.

"The mud affected the movement not only of infantry troops but also that of those Tiger tanks that, not resting on solid ground, ended up by bogging down. Our adversaries, however, who were in an area that was not flooded, could move their Shermans with great ease. The first days on the front were spent amid great difficulties in adapting; we sought to adapt to a situation that was far from easy. On March 29, I found myself in a foxhole with SS legionnaire Antonio Tosi, a lad from Palagano, in Modena Province. The situation around us seemed quiet enough, so, since I had just received a letter from a girl with whom I was in contact, I thought that I could read it in peace. I immersed myself in reading it, but a few seconds later, without taking my eyes off the paper, I got

A Brummbär assault gun passing by the damaged Tiger I

into some humorous banter with Tosi. In the same instant, a burst of machine gun fire from the Anglo-American lines zipped over our heads. Not getting any response from my companion, I turned toward him and saw that he was not moving. A stream of blood ran from under his helmet. A bullet had hit him in the head, killing him on the spot. The foxholes were more 50 meters [164 ft.] apart, while the front line was about 300 meters [984 ft.] from the enemy line, largely covered by mines. When night fell, we went out on patrol toward the enemy lines. One night, two SS legionnaires who had infiltrated the enemy positions began to gather information. Not much time passed before they were discovered by the British, who, after having disarmed them, shot them on the spot.

"The Americans were unquestionably more correct than their allies but did not show themselves in the front line. . . . On the night of April 13, we were supposed to go out on the usual round of patrols, but, because of the full moon, we had to cancel because we would have been exposed to great risk. Instead of

British prisoners captured by the Germans at the Anzio bridgehead, 1944

German prisoners captured at Anzio

American prisoners captured by the Germans being sent to the rear

German soldiers and Tiger tank in the Cisterna sector of Nettuno. *NA*

returning to camp straightaway, I decided to stop to see a couple of buddies with whom I had developed a friendship, who were on guard duty in a foxhole not too far away. Not much time passed before Hauptsturmführer Remo Buldrini showed up on an inspection round. As soon as he jumped into the foxhole, incoming covering fire began from the enemy lines. Meanwhile, the sky had clouded over. Buldrini, who had been in the war in North Africa and was familiar with combat techniques in the desert, told us to grab our weapons and to take up positions on the sides of the foxholes, ready to fire. The *Hauptsturmführer* took out his flare pistol and, pointing it upward, fired it. A few seconds later, the flare burst, lighting the sky like day. About 5 meters [16.5 ft.] from me, I saw an Indian soldier appear who, thanks to the covering fire, had reached the foxhole undisturbed to massacre us all. I had barely enough time to think and emptied the entire magazine against him. The chance arrival of Buldrini in the foxhole had saved my life. The next night, on April 14, in accordance to orders by an *Untersturmführer* whose name I prefer not to mention, Sturmmann Giuseppe Italiani; SS legionnaires Mario Biglino, Felice Casali, Oreste Ciavarella, and Vincenzo de Mayda; and I went on patrol toward the enemy lines. We reached Borgo Flora, a group of houses halfway between Borgo Podgora and Cisterna di Latina, where there was a forward post where we were supposed to meet some German engineers. They were to have shown us the exact path to follow, which was changed every day so that the minefield would be impossible for enemy patrols to cross.

"At Borgo Flora we found only one engineer, who informed the officer who was leading us that in the afternoon, his comrade had been wounded during a firefight with the Allies and had been brought to the Celio military hospital in Rome. He added that since he had not been able to find out what changes had been made to the minefield, it would be better for us to cancel our foray for that evening. Given that the previous night we had to stay in our own lines because of the bright moonlight, the *Untersturmführer* did not want any discussion and said that an Italian soldier was even capable of walking on mines. Unfortunately, his words were unknowingly prophetic. In fact, once he had given the order to follow him, he began walking toward the minefield. We moved in single file, and I was the last man. A few minutes later, we reached the place where there was supposed to be the gap that crossed the minefield, and we got in among the mines. It was not long before I heard an explosion. The blast of air threw me on the ground. At first I thought that the Anglo-Americans had spotted us and were firing on us with

A German patrol on a recon mission, near a flak gun hit by enemy fire

mortars, but then, not hearing any other explosions, I knew that someone had tripped a mine, making it explode. As I fell, I had been hit by some shell fragments. Two had gone into my leg, above the knee, and a third had broken a couple of teeth, and the fourth had hit me above my right eyebrow.

"Fortunately, none had hit any vital organs or cut any arteries. The sight I saw was dramatic. Despite the poor light, I recognized the shattered corpses of the other SS legionnaires. There was no trace of the *Untersturmführer*. Still in a state of shock, I backtracked and, limping, reached the headquarters. I reported to Buldrini and brought him up to speed on what had happened. Seeing me in that shape, the *Hauptsturmführer* said that he would see to recovering the bodies and any survivors and that I would be well advised to go to an aid station. I told him that I would go there after I had gone along with the recovery party to the scene of the explosion. I had to insist upon it before Buldrini agreed to my request. Once I had reached the spot, we tried to determine if there were any survivors. I saw Casali. There was a trickle of blood on his forehead. I thought he was wounded, but when we tried to make him come to, we saw that a fragment had hit him in the head, killing him instantly. Things were better with Biglino, who had lost a hand, and Italiani, who were the only survivors of the explosion, along with myself and, as I discovered a few days later, the *Untersturmführer* as well. As we were returning to camp, we ran into a squad of Anglo-American soldiers who, hearing the blast, had gone out on patrol to see what had happened. We got into a firefight to which I was only partially witness. In fact, given the amount of blood I had lost from my wounds, I soon lost consciousness. In the hours that followed, I had a few flashes of lucidity. Among these, I remember the moment in which I was brought to the field hospital tent, and the smell of ether with which the doctors put me to sleep."[4]

After about a monthlong stay at the Celio military hospital, Bortolotti was sent back home to continue to heal. He did not return to his battalion, stationed at Pinerolo, until summer 1944. In August of that year, the unit took part in Operation Nachtgall (nightingale) in the area between Pinerolo and Sestriere, to eliminate the local rebel bands: "The western area of Piedmont was involved in heavy fighting with the partisans from autumn of 1943. The partisans had been joined by groups of French partisans who were pressing up against our national border. Our employment in the area had been ordered to clear the zone of rebels and to relieve the French pressure."[5] During these early sweeps, Bortolotti soon learned that the partisans almost never fought in the open; they would fire a few rounds and then run off. During the time spent in Sestriere, clashes with the rebels were frequent. In early September, the SS unit was relieved by *alpini* from the Monterosa and returned to Pinerolo. Shortly after, the Degli Oddi Battalion was moved to Valcamonica for a new antipartisan operation. Bartolotti, who had been promoted to *Sturmmann* in charge of billeting, was then sent to Mariano Comense to find lodgings for his battalion. The headquarters took up residence in Villa Besana,

German defensive position in the Anzio-Nettuno bridgehead

Bortolotti, *second from the right*, at the top of Mount Fraiteve

Pinerolo, summer 1944: Giuseppe Bortolotti, *on the left*, with another SS legionnaire, Filippo Barese

and the *Stabskompanie* in the local elementary school. The area had been chosen because of the absence of rebel bands, which would make it possible to reorganize the battalion. Recommended for the Iron Cross First and Second Class by Waffen-Hstuf. Buldrini, to his great dismay, in the presence of Marshal Graziani (November 23, 1944), he was awarded only the Wound Badge in Gold. In February 1945, the new Waffen Grenadier Regiment der SS 81, commanded by the newly promoted *Waffen Standartenführer* Carlo Federigo degli Oddi, was moved to Val Trebbia in the province of Piacenza, to be employed not at the front against Allied forces, as the Italian volunteers had hoped, but in new sweeps. The regiment was attached to Kampfgruppe Binz: "On the morning of February 9, the day on which we left Mariano Comense, we paraded along the streets of the town, full of people who did not want to see us leave. When we reached Piazza Martiri della Libertà in the center of town, our passage was saluted by a shower of flowers. After some initial coolness, the people of Mariano had understood that we were soldiers who were fighting only for defense of the homeland."[6]

On February 16, Bortolotti's unit reached Bobbio, where battalion headquarters were set up. The various companies were sent to the surrounding towns, relieving troops of the 162. Turkestan-Infanterie-Division, whose behavior the German headquarters had complained of. There had also been many cases of desertion within the division. Bortolotti himself was involved in one of these cases: "On February 17, 5.Kompanie, to which I belonged, left Bobbio and went south, following State Road 45, which links Piacenza to Genoa, and headed toward Marsaglia, a small town in Val Trebbia about 10 kilometers [6 mi.] distant, where it was to relieve a company of 'Mongols.' Having reached the area of San Salvatore, about halfway there, near the bridge over the Trebbia, the advance guard found, hidden behind the low wall that ran along the roadside, a German lieutenant and his Turkmen orderly. . . . As soon as he realized that we were the Waffen-SS company that he was expecting, the lieutenant came out from behind the wall, met our commander, Waffen-Obersturmführer Aimone Ribolla, and brought him up how he and his orderly, the only one of his men who had stuck by him, had been able to miraculously escape from the 'Mongols' who had mutinied hours before and had joined the partisans. He also said that the men had taken up positions in the woods a few kilometers away and were waiting for us, knowing of our arrival, to ambush us. Ribolla ordered the legionnaires to deploy on the sides of the road, to wait until it got dark. . . . He split the company into three platoons. The first was to proceed along State Road 45, while the other two were to flank the group of 'Mongols' to their right and their left. The group I was in went down to the Trebbia, and after crossing the river we climbed up on the opposite ridge, well above the Turkmen. We reached our positions, and when the platoon that had advanced along the state road got to within firing range of the enemy positions and had engaged the enemy, we began to fire. The darkness prevented us from locating the exact enemy positions, and we ran the risk of firing on our own comrades. The tracer rounds acted well, thus, as position markers. The Turkmen company, finding itself unexpectedly in a crossfire, was unable to put up much of a fight and pulled back into the woods in haste, thus avoiding heavy losses. Having momentarily cleared the field, in the morning we entered Marsiglia but hardly had the time to secure the town when the 'Mongols,' along with a group of partisans from the GL 1st Division, launched a fresh attack. In the four days of battle that followed, we traded shot for shot and were finally able to push our adversaries out of the town, taking only one casualty in our ranks."[7]

Bortolotti's battalion remained in Bobbio until early March, then because of continual partisan attacks was moved to Perino, where the unit headquarters was set up. The companies were later deployed first along the Trebbia between Settima and Podenzano, a few kilometers from Piacenza, and then to Rivergaro, farther northeast. On April 16, the troops were sent to Momeliano di Gazzola to assist some Republican troops who had been surrounded. In the days that followed, with the deterioration of the military situation and the approach of Allied troops, the men of Kampfgruppe Binz were ordered to converge on Piacenza; Bortolotti's battalion was used to maintain a bridgehead south of the city to facilitate the withdrawal of other units. On April 28, 1945, following the retreat of the battalion toward Melegnano, Bortolotti, in civilian clothes and after having destroyed his *Soldbuch*, managed to avoid capture at a CLN roadblock by passing as an ex-prisoner who had escaped from a Todt worksite. Returning home to Pavia, he was picked up a few days later by members of the CLN and brought to the police headquarters and from there to the Castello Visconteo in Pavia, where a prison for political prisoners had been set up. Despite his having been a member of the Italian SS, he was able to save his life. Giuliano Bortolotti passed away on August 29, 2008, in Voghera.

Chapter XV

PASQUALE SCARPELLINO: WAFFEN-SCHARFÜHRER IN THE ITALIAN 29TH SS DIVISION

Scharführer Scarpellino of the II./81

A German paratrooper in Rome, 1943

Born in Formia (Latina) in 1925, at eighteen years of age, along with his brother and three friends from the Milizia Volontaria per la Sicurezza Nazionale, he reached the Anzio front with the desire to fight against the Anglo-American invaders. He joined the Italian SS, where he achieved the rank of sergeant for action in battle. His superiors recommended him to be awarded the Silver Medal for Military Valor in recognition of courage shown in combat during which he was severely wounded. Sent to the hospital, he was operated on several times.

Where were you on July 25, 1943?[1]
On July 25, 1943, I was assigned to the 115th Legion of the MVSN in Viterbo. Upon the announcement of Mussolini's arrest, some in the city were under the illusion that the war was over. They made us Blackshirts remove the fasces from our uniform lapels, replaced by stars. Mussolini's arrest, in my opinion, was something unplanned. Because although the war was not going well, Mussolini was liked by the people, no matter what they say today.

And the day of the announcement of the armistice?
On September 8, 1943, I was still in Viterbo, and even then, some people thought that there would be a quick end to the war. I remember the proclamation on the radio made by Badglio, the marquess of Sabotino, or, better yet, "of sabotage." On September 13, after Mussolini's speech on the radio, I went to Piazza delle Erbe and ran into a Blackshirt officer by the name of Satta, whose son would later be executed by the partisans at Schio, in the province of Vicenza. He was standing there, in his uniform and black shirt, almost as if to challenge all those who passed by him. I quickly went home and put on my black shirt and returned to give him support. A few fisticuffs flew with some subversives. I went to the Milizia headquarters in Via dell'Orologio Vecchio and was dumbfounded. Alongside some old Fascists, those of the early days, were many youths. Youths who, galvanized by Mussolini's speech, had flocked there. This fact impressed me a lot. Among others, I remember Benito Dragoni[2] and Bruno Dini, who was a volunteer along with me at Nettuno and, after the war, would become a doctor. Il Duce's speech, from Radio Munich, reinvigorated us, buoyed us all up. There is no doubt about it.

Who reopened the headquarters of the Viterbo Fascist Party?
The local Fascist party reopened and summed its vigor thanks to the actions of Giulio Catarcini, Fedele Giacci (a pharmacist), and Giuseppe Zampi, a lawyer. There was a climate of enthusiasm and of revenge. We were still there, still in place. We said to ourselves: "This great adventure is starting again. It's not over." We removed the stars and replaced them with the fasces on our lapels of our black shirts. I remember Consul Amadasi and Major Mineo.

Did the Milizia act as police in various communes in the province?
I remember the actions of the Milizia in Ischia di Castro, Farnese, and Valentano. The reactions that occurred, it must be said, were excessive. We sought out ambushes, stragglers, draft dodgers, but most of all we wanted to reaffirm that there was a constituted order, that the state of the RSI had its sovereignty. We gave a few slaps to those who had been reported as leaders on the opposite side, but no blood was shed.

Italian soldiers in civilian clothes on the outskirts of Rome, September 1943

Il Duce, Benito Mussolini

What about the partisans?

There wasn't even a shadow of the partisans. The subversives held many meetings and had ambitious projects, but there were no armed actions that I recall. At best, they distributed some leaflets or some newspapers among themselves. There were four or five high school students along with Buratti in Viterbo, but what did they accomplish? Nothing. What I didn't like was that they executed Buratti, who was a really great person. He had been my professor of Latin and Greek and had given me private lessons. He was from Bassano Romano, a good person; I respected him a lot. Then there were the *attendisti* (foot-draggers), those who didn't commit to either side and waited for the arrival of the Americans.

A German soldier and a young Fascist in Rome, September 1943

At some point . . .

We got tired of this situation. "What are we doing in Viterbo?" So we escaped. In fact, we were reported as deserters! All five of us headed to Rome. There was me, my brother Vincenzo, Bruno Dini, Aduo Vittori, all from Viterbo, and Guido Quaglia from Rome. We were those who were later described as "forward deserters" because we were not the only young Italians to leave everything in order to run to the front to fight. By hitching rides, we got to Rome. We had no lack of fun. We caroused around a bit. That evening, we saw a show with the Nava sisters, we of course went to the whorehouse, we ate well. We thought that we would have our fun before we went to the front. In a store, we bought a piece of black cloth, within a tricolor border. The center was inscribed with "*Per l'onore d'Italia*" ("For the honor of Italy"). We had it sewn on the sleeve of out Milizia jackets. We reached the front partially on foot and partially by hitching rides. The next day, we headed to the front itself on foot. Every once in a while, some "good soul" gave us a lift. We got to Cisterna on April 14, 1944. There we entered a wrecked house. There was a mirror, and we looked at ourselves and said, "Wow, how ugly we are." Resuming our march to the front, we ran across two Germans on a motorcycle and sidecar. We asked where the front was, and they brought us to an Italian unit, which then escorted us to the headquarters of II Battalion of the 1st Italian SS Regiment, commanded by Degli Oddi. We were welcomed warmly by the Italian SS, by Captain Comini and Lieutenant Bruno Minucci of Siena, the battalion adjutant. He asked us in wonder: "Why have you come here?"

Paratroopers of 2.Fallsch.Div. in Rome, September 1943

We replied, "We want to go to the front to fight." We wanted to join Prince Borghese's Decima MAS. Our comrades said that they would accompany us in a few days to the area of the front that was held by men of the Decima or of the Nembo, but they did not want to go to the front just then, and we asked to stay with them.

A German infantry unit passing through the town of Cisterna, spring 1944

A German soldier on the Lazio front

German soldiers and a Tiger tank on the streets of Cisterna, spring 1944

American troops in combat on the Anzio front, spring 1944

So then they recruited you in the Italian SS?
They "recruited" us in the 3rd Company and brought us to the front line in the Borgo Carso–Borgo Podgora sector and put us in the mortar platoon. We were later sent to the 2nd Platoon, led by Sergeant Giacomo Bellucci.[3] Each night, one of our patrols went out into no-man's land.[4] Once in a while we traded shots with the Americans and the British, who were also out on patrol. We also took prisoners, as they also did, and one night they captured one of our patrols.

One night I led the patrol, and the next night my brother led it, because we were the only two corporals, since we had retained our Milizia ranks. We were in the trenches, which often filled up with water. Morale was high, despite the great price in blood we had to pay every day. We still did not have the black tabs on our lapels, which were awarded us after the fighting at Nettuno.

How were your relations with your fellow soldiers?
The unit was composed, in part, of Italian soldiers who had been prisoners of the Germans in Germany and had then joined the RSI and returned to Italy. I remember a guy named Angelini. Most of my comrades were from northern Italy. They were in a unit commanded by Degli Oddi and had decided to stick with their commander. Degli Oddi had the standard of the Republic of Siena, I don't know how he got it; maybe he inherited it from his family. Degli Oddi often cited us as an example to our other comrades: "These boys left voluntarily"—he said to his soldiers—"and came to the front just to fight." Five youths who left the peace of their homes, to go to fight at the front, was surely an exceptional thing.

How were your relations with the Germans?

The relationship with our German comrades was excellent. At times they would come to our lines to speak with our commandant. They made the betrayal of September 8 weigh heavily on me. They treated us as if we were their own. Taken individually, the Germans were good soldiers, agreeable and very generous. But when they were in a group, there was no room for anyone else.

Tell us about your brother Vincenzo.

The Allies shelled our lines incessantly. On May 17, 1944, my brother Vincenzo went out on patrol and did not come back. In those days, the enemy, after an intense shelling, broke through our front, and I didn't see him anymore. I tried to go find him, but they stopped me because it was too risky. I don't know what fate he met. If he died there, [or] if he was taken prisoner. His body was never recovered. My sister looked for him for a long time. We got the strangest news, which then turned out to be unfounded. Someone had seen him as a prisoner in Afragola; someone saw him in Rome, put up against a wall and shot along with three Fascist youths. But it was not true.

When the front collapsed, did you retreat?

In the chaotic retreat, the rally point was set as Florence. We were to get there, as a group if possible. While we were retreating, Sergeant Giacomo Bellucci from Schegge (Perugia) gave me some fatherly advice: "Stop at Viterbo," he said. "Who's making you follow us to the north? Stay home; you're eighteen years old, if you stop here, who's going to say anything?" It was a father's advice rather than that of a soldier. In Rome, I lost contact with my comrades and couldn't find my unit. When I got to Viterbo, I found my home ransacked, completely destroyed by the bombings. Faced with that tragedy, I got into a rage and immediately afterward asked myself what end my family had suffered. The situation was difficult. My brother lost and probably wounded or dead; my father, who was a volunteer, was in the Balkans and was given up as missing. My mother and three sisters had taken refuge at the Urcionio,[5] where today a memorial plaza stands. When my mother asked about my brother, I did not have the courage to tell her the truth, and came up with a lie: "Vincenzo, bless him, was taken prisoner. The war is over for him."

In Viterbo, did you meet up with your comrades from the GNR ex-MVSN?

It was June 7; only a few remained in the Milizia barracks, only seven or eight comrades. A few days later, on the ninth, the Anglo-Americans arrived. Consul Cavina told us to take what we wanted out of the warehouse. I took some cured meats, some cold cuts, and brought them to my family. It was a feast. My mother and my sisters made a lot of friends among the people of Viterbo. They ate along with the other homeless people. I'm still happy today that I did what I did.

Did you decide to reach your unit in the north?

I was bent on going north. With two other friends, I set off for Florence. One of the two was from Montefiascone, and the other [was] from Acquapendente and thought it wise to stop off at home. Along the way, the Germans often stopped and gave me a ride. I had a strange uniform that resembled theirs a lot. I was also equipped as they were, armed with a machine pistol. Partly on foot and partly by hitching rides, I arrived in Florence by myself but couldn't find anyone. Along with a few Blackshirts of the 115th Legion, we got

A German patrol on the Anzio front, spring 1944. The soldier on the right is armed with a flamethrower.

A German defensive position on the Anzio front

A German flak position on the Anzio front, 1944

American tanks on the street in Rome, spring 1944

German soldiers captured by the Americans, May 1944

Piedmont, late spring 1944: A group of Italian NCOs of the Italian SS Legion. Most are still wearing the uniforms from their unit of origin, some still with the Regio Esercito side cap, with the new SS insignia with red background.

A "Public Order" company of the Republican National Guard

to Brescia. There was a GNR headquarters where a lot of stragglers were gathering; I spent some time with them. By asking around, I found out that my battalion was at Mariano Comense.

A surprise awaited you there.
In fact, as soon as I reached Mariano Comense, I was promoted to sergeant, for actions in battle. I took off my Milizia uniform that I was still wearing, and they gave me the appropriate uniform. To those who like me had been at Nettuno, they gave the black SS insignia. We trained a lot at Mariano Comense, even in the mud. We didn't carry out any major sweeps.

Do you remember the day they awarded the Silver Medal to your battalion's standard?
I remember the big show very well. It was November 23, 1944, and we were all in a field between Mariano Comense and Cantù. Marshal Graziani personally presented the Silver Medal for Military Valor, awarded by Il Duce to the battalion's standard. At the end of his speech, a deafening roar of "*Fronte! Fronte!*" was raised. We wanted to go fight the Americans.

And did they grant your wish?
They sent us to Rivergaro (in Val Trebbia in Emilia). We were to go to Garfagnana, but for reasons unknown we stayed there to carry out actions against the partisans. We were informed that at night they had attacked one of our barracks, and in the following days we carried out sweeps. We had contacts with the local populace. With some, who declared that they were proud to be partisans, we traded cigarettes and talked. They tried to convince us, and we told them to go back home. They even had me to dinner, but at a certain point I saw a movement that I did not like, and I left.

An Italian SS Legion NCO

Italian SS legionnaires during a training session

Then they billeted you in Perino?

We were quartered in a country school. We carried out investigative activities in civilian clothes in Perino (Piacenza). With Sergeant Moneta, awarded the Iron Cross at Nettuno, we tried to infiltrate the partisans. However, they caught on and took us prisoner. They tried to convince us to switch to their side. They made their reasons and we made ours. We were immovable. They were a group of young men guided by an older man. They were motivated by a hatred of the Germans. These partisans were not well liked by the locals because they lived by plundering the poor farmers in the area. They took cows and animals. The farmers were mad at the partisans, but afraid of them at the same time. We took advantage of a momentary distraction by our captors, and we took off as fast as we could. They fired on us, but thanks to God they were terrible shots and luckily did not hit us. Our garrison was a couple of kilometers away, and we got there in record time. They moved us from Perino. We were to go to the front. But at Rivergaro they stopped us; I don't know why.

Tell us about the day you were wounded.

On April 16, 1945, we carried out an action at Momeliano di Gazzola to rescue a company of Fascists from Mantova who were surrounded by the partisans. We surrounded a hill. The partisans were on top of it, holed up in the Castello di Monticello. While we advanced, an intense enemy machine gun fire began, and I tried to help a wounded officer.[6] I heard a loud bang and luckily remained conscious. They carried me away. It was a serious bullet wound to the right half of my chest. Luckily, the round went right through me. They brought me to the base of the hill, where I think there was a collection point for the wounded. I crossed the Trebbia River on a cart pulled by oxen, and they brought me to a hospital in Piacenza, where I was operated on in haste. Since the round had hit my lungs, I had emphysema and was swollen. They made a small cut to let the air escape. During the night of April 24, they brought me to Casalpusterlengo, and on the morning of the twenty-fifth to the Baggio Hospital in Milan. When I was recovering in the hospital in Como, there was a family from the Viterbo area that was staying in Cantù, and I contacted that family through a Red Cross nurse and gave them all of my most precious things: my Republican Fascist Party card, because I was registered with the

Banner of the 2nd Italian SS Regiment, November 1944

Italian SS legionnaires, November 1944

An Italian SS legionnaire. Note the right-hand tab with three arrows.

A group of partisans preparing an ambush

Italian SS Legion officers. *Borgatti*

Viterbo section, photos, and other things. However, the partisans often searched his house; my friend was afraid and threw everything away. I don't have anything anymore. Luckily my sister had saved one photograph.

Did the Germans ask you to go with them?
The Germans had permission to bring their wounded to Switzerland. Seeing that I was SS, my German comrades told me to go with them, because the wounded had this pass to go to Switzerland. I didn't have a shirt, and I had a country housewife's scarf embroidered with the word "Duce" all over it that was wrapped around my chest. It was a great piece of innocence.

When I got to Como, the partisans looked at the scarf and saw that I was Italian and made me get off the truck and dragged me, between spitting on and insulting me, to Caverlata (Como). I stayed in the hospital there and underwent a new operation.

You escaped the partisan massacres.
Every evening the partisans of the 52nd Garibaldi Brigade came by, with their red kerchiefs around their necks. They looked us over, took two or three of us, and carried them off. What end these comrades suffered, I don't know. It seems that they executed some in the courtyard of the hospital. As soon as my condition improved, they moved me to the jail of San Donnino in Como, but because there was no room, they brought me to a school converted to a jail, on Via XX Settembre. The daily paper *Il Popolo Comasco* wrote that the twisted figure Pasquale Scarpellino of the Italian SS had been put in jail. But who knew these people? Why a twisted figure? How did they know if I was twisted or not? From there, they transferred me to Abate, where I vacationed for a few months. Five or six months passed at Abate, and finally they sent me home with permit papers.

After the War

Having escaped the partisan massacres, Scarpellino returned to Viterbo, finding a city destroyed by bombings. In the postwar period, he attained a degree in the classics, attended university, and got a medical degree, becoming a respected surgeon. Pasquale Scarpellino passed away on December 19, 2009.

A partisan formation on the march, spring 1945

Two photos of Scarpellino during a 2009 interview

Chapter XVI

CIRILLO COVALLERO: AN ITALIAN IN THE SS-POLIZEI-DIVISION

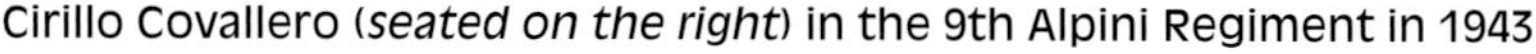

Cirillo Covallero (*seated on the right*) in the 9th Alpini Regiment in 1943

Italian soldiers after September 8

Italian soldiers in a German prison camp, autumn 1943

Cirillo Covallero was born in Torrebelvicino on July 11. 1922. In 1942, he entered the Gioventù Italiana del Littorio [*Translator's note*: an Italian Fascist youth organization, abbreviated GIL], receiving premilitary training. On September 12, 1942, he was called to arms, in the Vicenza alpine battalion. After having avoided being sent to the Russian front due to a supposed health problem, he was sent to Sant'Andrea di Gorizia and assigned to the 9th Alpine Regiment depot (Julia Division). He stayed there until September 8, 1943, when the news of the armistice arrived.

Let us hear Cirillo Covallero's direct testimony:[1] "I was there on September 8 when I heard the announcement of the surrender. I and everyone else shouted for joy, but a lieutenant calmed us down and said that for us, the war would start then. A 'little lieutenant' quickly called me, along with a sergeant, and about a dozen soldiers and we went to check the roadblock into the city. On the morning of the ninth, we arrived at the checkpoint at Salcano. There were fortified posts with heavy machine guns that controlled anyone who wanted to enter the city. At that moment there was a group of partisans with red flags, and a lot of women as well, and the lieutenant called me with the sergeant to go and stop these people who wanted to enter the city of Gorizia.... The lieutenant fired a burst into the air with his submachine gun, and they stopped... then with the rest of the patrol, we moved forward and dispersed everyone."

On September 12, 1943, along with many other Italian soldiers, Covallero was loaded onto a train that brought them to Allenstein,[2] to a prison camp. The next morning, all the prisoners were invited to join the Waffen-SS. A hundred or so Italians accepted the invitation, and among them was our Covallero: "In the morning, everyone was out in

Italian soldiers in a German prison camp, autumn 1943

Covallero wearing the SS uniform, 1943

the courtyard, where there were Germans, and one of them spoke Italian and asked us if we wanted to join the '*esse esse*.' There were those who muttered that the '*esse esse*' were assault battalions, and thought that if they were, to go and to jump to the other side, but I didn't have the courage to be the first to take a step forward. There was a first and then I was the second, and then others as well. We went into another shed; in all, there were about a hundred of us, and that day they gave us a lot to eat. Then the order came to leave for Missingher,[3] and they gave us food for two days and I ate everything right away . . . it took us four hours to get to Missingher. It was raining there, and I was hungry. . . . Later we went to a barracks where there were a lot of stalls without horses, and they put us there on the ground. . . . After twenty days in the stalls, they assigned me to a room that was heated, and the beds had white sheets . . . but it lasted only a few nights, then they gathered us all together outside in a field and someone who spoke Italian said that they needed fifty mechanics, and I quickly raised my hand and was quickly taken along with fifty others who raised their hands, and they gave me ten marks and we left right away for Buchenwald, accompanied by the Germans. Naturally, I ate the food right away, and the trip lasted two days and we arrived in Vaimar[4] . . . and after a few hours of walking on foot we arrived at the Buchenwald concentration camp."

After a comprehensive medical exam, Covallero was deemed fit for active service. In late November, the Italians in the camp were again assembled to select ironsmiths and carpenters. This time, Covallero volunteered to be a carpenter. Sent to Berlin, he was given a German uniform and a *Soldbuch*: "The next day, they dressed me as a German and photographed me for the "*Solbuc*" (*Soldbuch*), which was like a passport, and showed all the stuff I had been issued, and so I started live as a soldier. I was assigned to the 1st Company workshop, and the other carpenter to the 2nd Company, and I quickly began to ply my trade. The cook in my company, who naturally was German, first brought me to show me a truck that I had to work on to make a mobile kitchen, and then they brought me to a shop where there were woodworking machines that I had never before

Another photo of Cirillo Covallero with the SS uniform, taken in Berlin in December 1943

Tirnavos, Greece, summer 1944: Cirillo Covallero wearing the 4.SS-Polizei-Division summer uniform

seen. Once I finished the work, I also had to take lessons, always in German. They issued gas masks and closed us up in a hermetically sealed glass room and released the toxic gas. They made us understand that if the masks did not work, we had to break the glass and jump out, but everything went well. Then one day we went to a place across town on foot, because bombings had destroyed the road, to test our blood type. They took a little blood from our ear and analyzed it. I had type A, and they cut that beneath my arm and wrote it in the passport. . . . One day we went to the range to fire at a target with a German rifle, whose sights were different than our model 91 rifle, and we messed everything up; we couldn't even hit the target board . . . because we all missed the target, they had us do thirty push-ups as punishment. Then we learned what to do to and hit the bull's-eye. The Flying Fortresses came to bomb Berlin four days a week; they came at night around 2300.

"We took shelter in a tunnel that protected us, and between bombs and antiaircraft guns I was always left breathless. Once the alarm was over, my company and I went to bed except for whoever was on rescue duty. One night I had to do guard duty, and I saw a plane caught in the searchlight; it was a spectacle not to be forgotten, and it was targeted by the antiaircraft guns."

Transfer to Greece

In late December 1943, Covallero was transferred to the SS-Polizei-Division, then being reorganized, with its men scattered between the Balkan front and the Leningrad front. On December 25, Covallero was put on a train bound for Greece. The first stop was Budapest, then on to Larissa in Greece. The train took all of nine days because of attacks by Communist partisans: "To get to Larissa in Greece from Budapest it took nine days, with the danger that we might be blown into the air like other trains. We were about a hundred soldiers with about sixty vehicles. Of these hundred soldiers, thirteen were Italians from varying regions. Once we arrived in Larissa, we quickly went to work and set up a workshop in some sheds. There were a lot of machines that were not in working order, and we fixed them. We worked bare chested; it was early January 1944. Then from Larissa we were moved to Tirnavos, a town about 15 kilometers [9 mi.] from Larissa. . . . When we got there, there were hundreds of vehicles of all types and also motorcycles; there was a Benelli 250. . . . We had an hour a day of practice as to how to defend the camps, because if a tank managed to break through the front line, we were supposed to stop it with a *Panzerfaust*, Molotov cocktails, and magnetic mines. We trained with rifles, light machine guns, and gas masks. At first we worked with our masks on for half an hour a day, and then later up to three hours a day. They would throw tear gas, and we had to change our filters by ourselves; while the lenses were cleaned by a companion, because you had to keep your eyes closed and with a handkerchief over your mouth, you had to get down as close as you could to the ground with your face. In our jacket liners, we had all sizes of gauze bandages and disinfectant and a cloth for liquid gas and a small bottle of liquid in case of need.

Cirillo Covallero, *center with rifle*, with other Italian comrades of the SS-Polizei-Division, at rifle practice in Larissa, Greece, summer 1944

Men of the SS-Polizei-Division during a sweep

SS-Polizei-Division recon troops in Greece, summer 1944

Polizei soldiers in Greece, 1944

A Greek auxiliary, wearing an armband, providing information to officers of the Polizei-Division during an antipartisan operation

"That was a place in which malaria was prevalent; we had to take pills every day and not drink water, but only tea, which was readily available, and they gave me a lot of shots like I had never had anywhere else before. We were free in the evenings, but there was nothing to do in the town. The people were all shut up in their houses, and the young girls kept out of sight because those of us dressed like Germans scared them. . . . In early June of forty-four, we were ordered to go to the French front because the Allies had landed in France . . . but in the evening there was a counterorder direct from Hitler; we were not going to the French front. . . . Meanwhile, summer had come and they gave us summer uniforms; we were magnificent soldiers. . . . Then one day, some Italians, working with the partisans, placed some time-delay explosives in an ammunition depot located in the countryside. They ran off but one was caught and, after being beaten, said that at six in the evening, the depot would blow up, but that the explosives were hidden and he didn't know where they were; he only knew what time they were set to go off. I went into town anyway, but at six on the dot the first ammo started to blow up; they were large aircraft bombs that made the houses shake. The alarm was sounded, and all of us put on our helmets and grabbed our shovels and got onto a truck and headed to the depot. But nothing could be done; it was too dangerous, and we had to clear out. A lot of soldiers came and surrounded the town. It was a dark night, and a German and I took up a position this side of the river. The town was on the other side. . . . The ammunition depot took three days and three nights to finish exploding. . . . One Sunday in July, we went to the beach at the foot of Mount Olympus because the nearby river was dry and was of no use to us. Then the weapons repair company went, and while they were in the water the partisans showed up and massacred them. Thirty-three were absent at roll call, between dead and missing.

"We were ready in case of partisan attacks. At night, a whistle—partisan alarm—and in five minutes we were assembled outside with all available weapons pointed toward where the partisans were, and patrols were already moving. . . . Then in August my platoon followed the combat troops that were making sweeps. We had about twenty vehicles and always camped outside the city; there were about thirty of us soldiers, three were Italian, and we pitched our tent together because we had a cape with which we could put up a tent for two or for three. . . . We changed location every two or three days, with the vehicles camouflaged with olive branches, but fighter planes showed up out of nowhere and strafed us. . . . I don't remember the names of the places and the cities where I was; I remember only the city of Giannina. We made camp, as always, 6 or 8 kilometers [3.5–5.0 mi.] outside the city, and there were some houses not far off, and so we went out in full gear to search for partisans, but there were only old ladies working the tobacco to be seen.

Cirillo Covallero with his SS uniform in Como, October 1944

A parachute swimmer

Parachute swimmers of the Decima Flottiglia MAS

"After a few days we left by night, because enemy fighter planes were always over the roads, and there were many burned vehicles on the edge of the road. We stopped for two or three days wherever we went, and then we did the same job every time. Once we stopped in the mountains. The vehicles were stopped with about 50 meters [164 ft.] between each vehicle. There were about twenty trucks, and the column was about a kilometer [0.6 mi.] long. . . . That morning, we started to move with the trucks. It was a nice day, and before my eyes was the sea. We came down from the mountain along a road that ran along the sea, but after a few kilometers the column stopped because we got the order to move to the Russian front; the Carpathians were our destination."

Return to Italy

Returning to the camp at Tirnavos, Covallero got orders to transfer to Germany. He left Larissa by train, passing through Thessaloniki and Serbia, reaching Vienna in late September. After a few days, still in the SS-Polizei-Division uniform, he was sent to the camp at Buchenwald and from there, with other Italians, got orders to return to Italy: "Then they sent me to Italy with twenty other soldiers, destination Pinerolo. I boarded a train in Weimar, full of tanks. Upon arrival in Munich in Bavaria, the alarm sounded and smoke was generated at the station. . . . At Pinerolo there were Italian SS troops commanded by German officers, and from there they sent me, with fifty other soldiers, to Alzate in Brianza, Como Province. We were billeted in a large shed, and our job was to clean up a villa, with a fenced-in park, that was to be used by the German commanders, and we had to pull guard duty. I was still in my German uniform . . . I spent a couple of months there, let's say well. The locals spoke with us; there were no partisans . . . someone told me that we could escape to Switzerland. He was a smuggler and knew how to plan an escape. There were four of us, and we decided to do it, and at a certain point he told us to wait for him and he went forward with another guy, and we never saw them again. Then my friend, who was a Neapolitan, and I went to take refuge with the Decima MAS, saying that we were Italians and that we didn't want to stay with the Germans."

The four "deserters" then went to Casaco, where there was a Decima MAS headquarters; they were assigned to the N.P. Battalion (parachute swimmers of the Decima Flottiglia MAS) and were issued a uniform and equipment, along with a blanket and a mattress. Thus ended Covallero's adventure as a Waffen-SS combatant. He ended the war still fighting with the Decima MAS. Cirillo Covallero died on February 5, 2009.

Assault guns of SS-Pz.Abt.4 of the SS-Polizei-Division in the streets of Thessaloniki, spring 1944

Chapter XVII

SEPTEMBER 8 FOR RUTILIO SERMONTI, IN GREECE

Sermonti in his Italian uniform

Blackshirts on the Greek front during an official ceremony

The Thermopylae area in a photo of the 1941 campaign

Map of the Thermopylae area

Rutilio Sermonti, Italian historian, politician, and zoologist, was born in Rome on August 18, 1921, the son of Alfonso Sermonti, a lawyer whose origins were in Pisa, who specialized in labor law and nationalization of the economy. During the Second World War, Rutilio first served in the Piave motorized division, and then as a Regio Esercito second lieutenant in the 24th Infantry Division Pinerolo on the Balkan front. The Pinerolo was in Thessaly, Greece, starting in June 1941, employed as an occupation force and in operations against Greek partisan bands. Antipartisan operations continued until September 8, 1943, when the news of the armistice with the Allies was announced. In those days, lieutenant Sermonti led an antipartisan detachment that was subordinate to 4.SS-Polizei-Panzergrenadier-Division, near Thermopylae.

While most of the Pinerolo division decided not to turn over their weapons to the Germans,[1] Sermonti decided to continue to fight alongside the SS units. Following is his testimony: "It was September 8; we had a clash with the Greek partisans and were returning to our base. There were seventy-six of us, part of a special formation created by our headquarters to fight against the partisan bands in the region. An SS company marched along with us, and they were all very young. They marched ahead of us; we were a bit behind. We got close to the pass at Thermopylae. The young SS troops went ahead, when all of a sudden, stones began to rain down from the surrounding heights, hurled down by the partisans. While the German soldiers sought shelter, some of our guys climbed up the mountain, forcing the Greek rebels to fall back so that we were able to resume our advance with no further incidents. Because it had become dark, we decided to make camp before returning to our base, since our headquarters had ordered us never to return at night. This was because the partisans had learned our signal codes with our flares, and there could be problems. The Germans camped along with us. A lieutenant named Meyer led them, a South Tyrolean who spoke Italian very well. At that moment the news of the armistice reached us, and my men were happy to hear it. I asked them what they were so happy about. If the war is finished now, it means we lost it; you know what the situation is on the various fronts, right? Within a few minutes they all understood the seriousness of the situation. During the night, a runner from headquarters arrived with an absurd order: disarm the German soldiers. But how? I asked the messenger. The Germans are sleeping among my own men; am I supposed to whisper the order in their ears and tell them to take the weapons from their comrade next to them? Fortunately, a few hours later Meyer and his young SS troopers left us, and we remained to await new orders. . . . Shortly afterward, a small truck of ours got there with a chubby NCO on board, who ordered me to turn over my pistol since I had been put under arrest, and that I would be subject to a court-martial because I had disobeyed an order from our headquarters. Nothing came of it; I told him to go back where he came from and that we would never give up our weapons. After a few hours, Meyer returned with his SS men, in turn asking me to turn our weapons over to them; in a very friendly manner, I let him know that we, with the armistice in force, thousands of kilometers from the homeland, never but never would give up our weapons. I also had with me veteran soldiers who were very experienced and had nothing to fear from the really young SS troopers. We thus asked to keep our weapons, pledging our loyalty and our strong desire to continue to fight alongside them."

During his service with the SS-Polizei-Division, Sermonti was awarded the Iron Cross Second Class. In 1944, he returned to Italy, serving as an officer in the 3rd Naval Infantry Division San Marco.

Sermonti in a 1944 photo

After the War

After the war, Sermonti got a law degree and worked in forensics. At the same time, he got involved in politics, becoming one of the founders of the Movimento Sociale Italiano [*Translator's note*: abbreviated as MSI, the Italian Social Movement was a neofascist and post-Fascist political party]. He left the party in 1956, returning again in 1969 along with Pino Rauti. Along with Rauti, in the 1970s he wrote a multivolume history of the Fascist Party. In 1995, after the disbanding of the party, he joined Pino Rauti's Movimento Sociale—Fiamma Tricolore (Social Movement—Tri-Color Flame) and, two years later, played a role in founding the Fronte Nazionale (National Front) political movement [*Translator's note*: both the Tri-Color Flame and the National Front were far-right political parties]. Considered by many to be one of the leading intellectuals of the Right, he had a following of many young people, to whom he often recounted an anecdote about a young German volunteer who, about to die from his wounds, raised his fist and shouted "*Niemals*" (never) as a show of his will and determination to never surrender in the face of the enemy or to life's adversities. Rutilio Sermonti passed away on June 14, 2015, at the age of ninety-three.

Sermonti in one of his last photos. *www.azionetradizionale.com*

CROCI DI FERRO

Dal fronte di Nettuno è giunta la seconda lista. Altri ventitrè dei nostri sono caduti e se agli altri possono sembrare pochi in paragone ai massacri di questa guerra, a noi sembrano moltissimi. Ventitrè commilitoni di settembre, ventitrè compagni che non hanno mai esitato e che, sin dal giorno più nero della Storia d'Italia, si sono schierati coi soldati del Reich per l'onore del popolo italiano e per la rinascita della Patria, hanno suggellato col sangue e colla vita il loro spontaneo giuramento. Eravamo in pochi, in settembre — non è vero, Legionari? — ed è ora per noi assai doloroso vedere le nostre file assottigliarsi. Che questo dovesse accadere lo sapevamo anche prima, perchè era nell'ordine logico delle cose per chi aveva preferito il morire in battaglia al vivere nella vergogna. Tuttavia ci duole, perchè non saranno più con noi a sognare una Italia gloriosa e potente, a cantare le canzoni della nostra gente; con loro non potremo più ridere e combattere. Anche questi ventitrè commilitoni, come quelli della prima lista, sono morti discretamente, quasi alla chetichella, anche se il nemico si è duramente accorto di averli contro. Nessuno ne parla. E veramente essi si erano arruolati volontari non per amore di propaganda o di encomi, ma per amor di Patria. Il sacro suolo di questa nostra Italia li ha amorevolmente accolti. Ed essi camminano ora nelle immense schiere della Legione dei Morti. Hanno formato un reparto isolato e marciano lungo gli interminabili sentieri dell'immortalità, fieri del dovere compiuto e delle loro belle mostrine rosse. E Mölders, che è il comandante della Legione, domanda loro: « Be' chi siete? Da dove venite? ». E quelli rispondono: « Siamo soldati d'Italia, comandante, siamo della SS. E veniamo da Nettuno ». E Mölders dice: « Venite con me, in prima fila. Perchè voi siete la più bella avanguardia della rinascente Italia ». E così camminano, fianco a fianco coi più famosi eroi d'Italia e di Germania, i nostri Legionari. E non si stancano, perchè sono diventati immortali, come l'Idea per la quale han no dato la vita. Questa Idea si chiama « Patria, Fede, Fedeltà ».

A questi ventitrè nomi, sono da aggiungere quelli dei dispersi, che sono rimasti sul campo feriti oppure morti. Nessuno di loro si è dato prigioniero, questo lo sappiamo benissimo, perchè la parola arrendersi non esiste nel vocabolario della Legione. Noi speriamo che essi siano ritornati alla conoscenza in un ospedale nemico, e lo speriamo perchè siamo certi che domani, nel doloroso campo di concentramento, essi sapranno tener alta la fiamma della loro passione fra i compagni di sventura.

Dallo stesso settore del fronte ci giunge notizia che altri due volontari della Legione SS Italiana sono stati decorati sul campo della Croce di Ferro di II Classe. Sono così sette i nostri commilitoni che hanno ricevuto, di fronte a un drappello d'onore germanico e a uno italiano, il riconoscimento del loro valore. Sette Croci di Ferro tutte nostre, e che resteranno nostre, della Legione SS Italiana, qualunque cosa dicano, facciano o scrivano gli altri.

Croci dei piccoli cimiteri di guerra, accanto allo scalo di Littoria, a Doganella, a Sermoneta; croci al valore, le une e le altre create attorno alla Legione la fulgida aureola dell'onore e della gloria che noi vogliamo un giorno protegga l'Italia dall'insulto del nemico e dello straniero come dal disprezzo dei posteri.

Proprio in questi giorni cade il 9 maggio, l'anniversario dell'Impero. Otto anni or sono lo festeggiammo sull'arsa sabbia rossa di Addi Abbi, fra Camicie Nere. Eravamo stanchi, laceri perchè la dura vita e il clima terribile del Tembièn ci avevano a poco a poco « messi a terra ». Non è vero, Generale Somma? Non è vero, Generale Diamanti? Ma quanta gioia e quanto orgoglio fra i camerati della « 28 Ottobre »! Ora non ci sembra possibile che in otto anni una così bella realtà abbia potuto diventare un sogno. Occorre che tutti ritornino a quella mentalità, a quella concordia che regnava nella nostra magnifica Divisione di Ventura, nei cui ranghi erano uomini di pura fede, erano giovani amanti d'avventure, erano strani tipi saltati fuori da chissà mai dove, erano giovani e vecchi, iscritti al Partito e non iscritti, tutti uniti nel sogno di una Italia grande, potente, imperiale.

Le Croci che brillano al sole delle terre Pontine sono un simbolo della rinascita, così come lo sono stati, uno per uno, nell'ormai lontanissimo mese di settembre, i volontari della Legione SS Italiana che senza nulla chiedere hanno offerto alla Patria e alla Causa il loro sangue e la loro vita come pegno di Fedeltà.

* * *

Il sangue dei volontari della Legione SS Italiana costituisce il riscatto dall'onta di Vittorino e di quella canaglia di Badoglio.

Onore alla Legione!

Un neo-volontario della Legione, il caporal maggiore Giovanni Draghi, dopo averci raccontato in una lettera come e perchè avesse comperato un numero di « Avanguardia » e lo avesse letto, ci scrive: « *Come potevo io bersagliere, con oltre sette anni di servizio in detto corpo — 6 mesi di Croazia e 13 di duro fronte russo — due volte ferito e decorato di medaglia d'argento al V. M. sul campo, restare in..., anzichè arruolarmi volontario?* ». E conclude: « *Come vedi, caro direttore, se da qualche giorno indosso la gloriosa divisa delle SS, oltre che al mio amor patrio, lo devo anche al tuo patriottico giornale* ».

Più bella lettera non potevamo ricevere. Nessun premio più grande. Risvegliare nelle ipnotizzate coscienze degli italiani il senso d'amor patrio è proprio il compito che ci siamo prefissati quando abbiamo pensato di creare questo settimanale.

Il caporal maggiore Draghi non è stato a farsi tante domande: ha obbedito al grande appello, con lo stesso animo, con lo stesso cuore, con la stessa fede che hanno guidato, in tanti anni di gloriosa carriera, il Maresciallo Graziani.

Che importa il resto, quando la Patria è in pericolo? Avanti tutti, italiani. Finitela di vivere nella paura della cartolina precetto. Presentatevi spontaneamente agli uffici di arruolamento, ai vostri distretti per combattere e per lavorare, per dare il vostro contributo alla ricostruzione morale e politica della nostra Italia! E date una precedenza agli uffici di arruolamento della Legione SS Italiana. Ma prima di decidervi ricordate bene questo: nella Legione esistono solamente doveri, perchè i diritti si conquistano sul campo di battaglia; nella Legione è proibito lamentarsi, perchè chi si lamenta non è degno di essere un SS; nella Legione bisogna obbedire ciecamente perchè nessuna colpa è più grave della disobbedienza. Ed ancora ricordate che oggi la SS è un ordine europeo e che dal momento del vostro arruolamento sino alla fine dei vostri giorni voi avrete fratelli tedeschi, francesi, valloni, belgi, olandesi, norvegesi, danesi, spagnoli, ucraini, lettoni ed estoni, questi ultimi da mesi duramente impegnati contro il bolscevismo. Ma soprattutto pensate che il vostro passato non deve più esistere per voi come non esiste per la Legione sino al giorno nel quale, paghi del dovere compiuto, voi farete vittoriosi ritorno alle vostre famiglie e ai vostri doveri di cittadini.

E un' altra cosa dovete ascoltare. La SS è una milizia scelta, è una milizia d'onore e di fede, non è — come vorrebbero far credere i nostri nemici (che sono poi i nemici dell'Italia, cioè gli ebrei, i massoni e i... simpatizzanti) — una specie di Ghepeù mascherata. La Legione SS Italiana è composta esclusivamente di truppe combattenti, di soldati che hanno giurato, per la vita e per la morte, di restituire all'Italia il suo onore, la sua indipendenza e i suoi confini.

* * *

One of the many drawings by Gino Bocccasile depicting the SS legionnaires in battle

ENDNOTES

Chapter I

1. Feldkommandostelle-SS Tgb Nr.35/128/23 g.

2. Divisions consisting of German citizens.

3. It officially assumed that designation on October 22, 1943.

4. Seriously wounded, he was repatriated to Italy and assigned as an instructor at the Rodengo-Saiano range of the Italian SS Legion. Promoted to *Oberscharführer*, Benedetti died in 1947 at the age of twenty-two because of wounds he had sustained in Russia. Information extracted from Sergio Corbatti and Marco Nava, *Karstjäger! Guerrilglia e controguerriglia nell'OZAK, 1943–45* (Seregno, Italy: Associazione MADM-Brianza Viva, 2005), 47n5.

5. For Gandini's military experiences, refer to the book by Francesco Paolo D'Auria, *Einer von Millionen: Ferdinand, la mascotte della Leibstandarte* (Milan: Mursia, 2011).

6. Marco Novarese, "Volonatari italiani nelle Waffen-SS," *La Legione* 4 (1999).

7. According to historian Carlo Gentile (*Le SS di Sant'Anna di Stazzema: Azioni, motivazioni e profilo di un unità nazista*), there were at least fifteen Italians, parceled out among the various units of the division, both combat and service, with various duties.

Chapter II

1. Except for the I./2 and III./2, but reinforced by III./SS-Art.Rgt. and 5.Bttr./SS-Flak.Abt.

2. It lacked its I./1 but was reinforced by II./SS-Pz.Rgt., by I./SS-Art.Rgt., by 12.(Kan.)/SS-Art.Rgt., by 4.Bttr./SS-Flak.Abt., and by the bulk of the SS-Pz.Jäg.Abt.

3. Ralf Tiemann, *Chronicle of the 7.Panzer-Kompanie, 1. SS-Panzer Division Leibstandarte* (Atglen, PA: Schiffer Military History, 1998), 71.

4. D'Auria, *Einer vin Millionen*, 173–79.

Chapter III

1. Feldkommandostelle SS Tgb. Nr.35/143/43 g.

2. Peter Hansen was born on November 30, 1896, in Santiago, Chile, son of a munitions plant manager. After the death of his father in 1903, his mother decided to return with the family to Germany. On September 1, 1914, he enlisted in the 48th Saxon Royal Artillery Regiment, serving in that unit throughout the First World War. In 1916, he was promoted to lieutenant and was awarded numerous decorations for valor shown on the battlefield. At the end of the war, Hansen joined the German Freikorps, engaged against the Communists in the Baltic countries. In 1922, he transferred to the 100,000-man Reichswehr army, spending the next twelve years in the rank of *Oberleutnant*. In April 1933, he joined the NSDAP (card number 2 860 864) and soon thereafter joined the SS (card number129 846). Between April 1933 and August 1935, he was assigned to SS-Oberschnitt Mitte. He returned to the army in August 1935 with the rank of *Hauptmann*, becoming a battery commander first at Naumberg, then in Leipzig, and finally in Meissen in 1937. Soon after, he was transferred to the army's 50th Artillery Regiment in Leipzig, commanding the *schwere* (heavy) *Abteilung* until January 1939. Promoted to major, he assumed command of II Abteilung / Artillerie Regiment 50. On June 1, 1939, he transferred to the SS-Verfügungstruppe (SS-Nr. 129 846), achieving the rank of *SS-Obersturmbannführer*. Because of his extensive experience in artillery units, he was given the mission to supervise the formation of the SS-VT artillery regiment at Juteborg. On August 10, 1939, the new SS-Artillerie-Regiment was incorporated into Panzer Division Kempf for employment in the Polish campaign. On January 30, 1942, he was promoted to *Brigadeführer*. From February 25 to May 1943, he supervised the formation of the Latvian Legion. He reached Italy in February 1944, taking charge of the integration of various Italian SS units into the new 1. Sturmbriagde. In early simmer 1944, he was designated as artillery commander (*ArKo*) of III./SS-Pz.Korps. In August 1944, he transferred to I./SS-Pz.Korps with the same post. In February 1945, he was transferred as chief of staff of XIII.SS-Armee-Korps, a post held until the end of the war.

3. Gustav Lombard was born on April 10, 1894, in Spiegelberg, SS-Nr. 185 023. In May 1940, as an *Obersturmbannführer*, he was *Chef* of 3./Kav.Rgt.1. Starting in January 1944, with the rank of *Standartenführer*, he took command of SS-Kav.Rgt.15, and in August 1944, promoted to *Oberführer*, he assumed command of 6.SS-Geb.Div., and beginning in October 1944, of the 31.SS-Frw.Gr.Div. In April 1945, he was promoted to *Brigadeführer*.

4. Johann Eugen Corrodi was born on August 18, 1897, in Gossau, near Zurich, Switzerland. In July 1940, he moved to Germany and joined the Waffen-SS (SS-Nr. 450 700) under the name of von Elfenau. Thanks to his previous military experience in the Swiss army, he taught military tactics at the SS-Junkerschule at Bad Tölz from November 1941 until April 1942, with the rank of *Sturmbannführer*. In May 1942, he was transferred to the SS-Kavallerie-Brigade as a staff officer. In January 1943, he assumed temporary command of SS-Kavallerie-Regiment 3.

5. Paolo De Maria was born on October 30, 1891, in Alessandria. He took part in the First World War as an infantry officer. He was wounded in combat three times. He was decorated with the Bronze Medal for Military Valor for engagements on August 6, 1916, during the Seventh Battle of the Isonzo. In 1921, he founded the Fascist Combat Group in Cori in Lazio, and the next year he took part in the March on Rome. The following year he joined the cadre of the Milizia Volontaria per la Sicurezza Nazionale (Volunteer Militia for National Security), where he attained the rank of consul general. He took part in the war against Ethiopia in a Blackshirt legion as a volunteer. He was later placed in a reserve status, but De Maria opposed that status and, after having won two appeals on July 8, 1941, and October 27, 1942, was allowed to return to service. On June 14, 1943, at Drnis in Yugoslavia, Consul De Maria assumed command of the 89th CC.NN. Assault Legion Etrusca, based at Volterra.

6. Constantin Heldmann was born on March 7, 1893, at Detmold/Lippe. He joined the SS in March 1933 (SS-Nr. 59 138), assuming command of SS-Standarte 22. At the same time, he was also serving in the army as an artillery officer. When the war began, he passed into the Waffen-SS with the rank of *SS-Hauptsturmführer* and was designated as commander of a battery of the SS-Artillerie-Ersatz-Abteilung. In January 1944, he was

assigned to the Wiking, in command of IV./Art.Rgt.5. In January 1942, he took command of the *Abteilung* of the artillery regiment of the SS Nord division. After having held other posts in Germany and on the Finnish front, in March 1943 he was assigned to Italy.

7. In late April 1944, when the 1.Sturmbrigade became the Waffen-Grenadier-Brigade der SS, the Italian volunteers were authorized to wear the black collar insignia. In Tagesbefehl Nr.65, SS-Ogruf. Wolff, in addition to granting the Italian volunteers the black collar insignia, also authorized that a special symbol, not yet specified, could be placed on the right collar tab by those who had fought at the front. In any case, the Italian volunteers continued to wear the black collar insignia without any symbol on the right, while the red insignia continued to be worn by personnel in training units.

8. Piero Mannelli was born in 1896 in San Romano, in the province of Pisa. He participated in the First World War as a lieutenant. He followed D'Annunzio in the Fiume episode and took part in the March on Rome. On February 1, 1923, he joined the Milizia. He took part in the Ethiopian campaign and in the expedition in Spain. At the beginning of the Second World War, he fought on the Greek-Albanian front and in North Africa. After having thrown his lot in with the RSI, in December 1943 he became subordinate to Generalleutnant Canavari and was put in charge of supervising the formation of Italian SS units.

9. Erich Tschimpke was born on March 11, 1898, in Breslau, SS-Nr. 40 065.

Chapter IV

1. The brigade, and later division, Reichsführer-SS traced its origins to the Begleit-Bataillon-Reichsführer-SS, formed on May 15, 1941, as an escort for the commander in chief of the SS, Heinrich Himmler. The battalion had been formed at Oranienburg, near Berlin. In September of that same year, the battalion was transferred to the Eastern Front in the Kalitino sector, about 60 kilometers (37 mi.)southwest of Leningrad. The unit was attached to the 2.SS-Infanterie-Brigade, at that time positioned on the right wing of the 18.Armee of Heeresgruppe Nord. From July 1942 until February 1943, the battalion was placed at the disposal of the *Reichsführer's* staff, the Kommandosstab-Reichsführer-SS. During that period, some of its personnel participated in operations against Soviet partisans in the area around Zhitomir, west of Kiev, during August 1942, and then in the Slavestno area from November 2 to 11, and in the Brazin area from November 9 to 14. Beginning in the month of December, the battalion was reorganized with new personnel at the Arys training camp and on February 15, 1943, was transformed into the Sturmbrigade Reichsführer-SS. At the end of February, the brigade was sent to France to the Rennes training area, then was put at the disposal of Army Group West until June. At the beginning of July, the brigade was sent to Corsica by sea and subordinated to the commander in chief of the German forces on the island (Wehrmachtsbfehlshaber Sardinien und Korsica), Generalleutnant Fridolin von Senger und Etterlin. Following the September battles against the French and Italian forces, the brigade retired from the island on October 4, 1943, then being assigned to the area between Trieste, Ravenna, and Ancona. At the end of the month, most of the personnel were pulled from the Italian front and sent to Slovenia, around the capital of Ljubljana. Between November and December, thanks to the arrival of the SS-Panzergrenadier-Leherregiment and personnel from other Waffen-SS formations, by order of the SS-FHA, transformation of the unit into a new armored grenadier division was begun (AMT II org. Abt. Ia / II Tagesbefehl Nr. 1565.43 g.Kdos, dated October 19, 1943), the 16.SS-Pz.Gr. Division Reichsführer, based on two regiments of *Panzergrenadieren*, numbered 35 and 36.

2. August Dietrichs, born on June 29, 1903, SS-Nr. 257 500.

3. Fritz Knöchlein, born May 27, 1911, SS-Nr. 87 881.

4. Herbert Vetter, born August 5, 1912, SS-Nr. 12 748.

5. Karl Diebitsch was born on January 3, 1899, in Hanover. During the First World War, he served in the Kriegsmarine. After the war, he joined the Freikorps to fight against the Bolsheviks. In 1934, he joined the SS (Nr. 141 990). With the rank of *Untersturmführer*, he was appointed as a cultural consultant and head of the SS Office for Artistic Matters, later becoming manager of the SS porcelain factory at Allach. Diebitsch was one of the chief designers of SS uniforms and insignia. In 1940, with the rank of *SS-Standartenführer*, he was assigned as commander of II./SS-Totenkopf-Standarte 11. In January 1942, he was posted to the Wiking, where for several days he commanded the Westland regiment before assuming command of SS-Flak-Abteilung 5. At the end of 1942, he was badly wounded in the head. Following a long convalescence, he was assigned to the staff of III.SS-Panzer-Korps in 1943 and later was designated as commander of the artillery regiment of the SS Nederland brigade. On December 1, 1943, he was posted to the staff of the Reichsführer SS, later becoming the chief of staff of 1.Sturmbrigade. Between March and June 1944, he commanded the *Kampfgruppe* of the Italian SS engaged on the Anzio front.

Chapter VI

1. Lothar Debes, born on June 21, 1890, in Eichstätt, SS-Nr. 278 953.

2. Alois Thaler, born on November 28, 1909, SS-Nr. 347 172.

3. Otto Jungkunz, born on July 23, 1892, in Würzburg, SS-Nr. 21 765.

4. Friedrich Noweck, born on August 5, 1914, in Danzig, SS-Nr. 429 633.

Chapter VII

1. Order of the SS-Führungshauptamt Tgb. Nr.1698/45 g., dated February 10, 1945.

2. Siegrfried Binz, born on March 13, 1898. Awarded the German Cross in Gold in 1943, as commander of I./Pol.Inf. Rgt.23.

Chapter VIII

1. Order of SS-Führungshauptamt Nr. 2045/44 g.Kdos, dated July 18, 1944.

2. Mainly South Tyroleans, Romanians, and Yugoslavs.

3. Odorico Borsatti was born on June 12, 1921, in Pola. A cavalry officer in the Regio Esercito, after September 8 he joined the Italian SS Legion, assigned as an adjutant to Generalleutnant Emilo Canevari, before being transferred to the OZAK and the Karstjäger Division.

4. Werner Hahn, born on October 2, 1901, in Krischow, SS-Nr. 23 546.

5. On January 30 (or January 29, but both dates are uncertain), Hitler instituted the Bandenkampfabzeichen, literally the badge for the fight against the bandits or badge for the fight against guerrillas. It was officially designated as the Kampfabzeichen

der Waffen-SS und Polizei; that is, the Combat Medal of the Waffen-SS and Police. It was the only military decoration of the Third Reich awarded specifically to members of the Waffen-SS. In addition, it was not conferred in the name of the supreme commander of the Wehrmacht, as was the custom for all German military awards, but was attributed in the name of the *Reichsführer-SS*. The badge was also instituted to make a clear distinction between the troops engaged on the front lines and those engaged in antiguerrilla warfare. It existed in three versions: bronze, silver, and gold, for 20, 50, or 100 days of combat. The medal for combat against the partisan bands could be awarded to all officers, NCOs, or soldiers engaged in antiguerrilla operations.

Chapter IX

1. With the ordinances of November 6, 1943, and January 7, 1944, Franz Hofer decreed obligatory military service in the Operationszone Alpenvorland.

2. A linguistic minority in the Dolomites, settled in the valleys that surround the imposing Sella massif; Val Badia, Val Gardena, Val di Fassa, Livinallongo, and Cortina d'Ampezzo. This population, which inhabited the Alps before the Roman conquest, adopted the Latin language, which, with the passing of generations, transformed itself into "ladino" (Ladin).

3. Lorenzo Baratter, *Le Dolomiti del Terzo Reich*, (Milan: Mursia, 2005), 249–50.

4. Ibid.

5. Ibid.

6. Ibid.

7. Earlier historiography often erroneously assigned titles to this division such as "Böhmen und Mähren," "Batschka," and others. In reality, in only a few cases was this unit referred to as SS-Division Lombard, named after its commander.

8. Helmut Gantz, born on December 12, 1910, in Kiel, SS-Nr. 425546. He had previously served in 30.Waffen-Gr.Div. der SS.

9. Hans von Ahlfen, *Der Kampf um Schlesien, 1944–1945* (Stuttgart: Motorbuch Verlag, 1991).

10 Lorenzo Baratter, *Le Dolomiti del Terzo Reich* (Milan: Mursia, 2005), 253.

Chapter X

1. The Italian unit was considered a Waffen Division der SS because it consisted of "non-German" volunteers not of German ethnicity who could not wear the double-rune insignia, and there was also a difference in ranks: the personnel of this formation used the prefix *Waffen* and not SS. Thus a *Hauptsturmführer* of the 29.SS was a *Waffen-Hauptsturmführer* and not an *SS-Hauptsturmführer*.

2. All candidates for Waffen-SS officers, called *Führerbewerber* (FB) and identified with a single stripe with two laces on the shoulder tab, underwent four months of training, after which they became cadet officers, a *Führerwärter* (FA) with the title of *SS-Junker* with a rank equivalent to an *SS-Unterscharführer*. They then attended a six-month command course, at the end of which they were promoted to the rank of *SS-Standartenjunker*, equivalent to an *SS-Hauptscharführer*, authorized to wear the cord on the cap, the belt, and the aluminum officer insignia on the collar. They were then sent to their units, where, after a minimum of two months, they were promoted to *SS-Untersturmführer*.

Chapter XI

1. Pio Filippani-Ronconi, "La 29a divisione granatieri SS," *Arthos* IV, I, no. 7/8 (January–December 2000).

Chapter XII

1. Born in Milan on April 17, 1927, died December 11, 2015.

2. Operation Hochland ("plateau") was planned in early January 1945. It called for a large sweep in the Valsesia and Biella areas and later along the hills between Lake d'Orta and Lake Maggiore. The main goal was to keep the partisan bands, in particular the Garibaldi formations led by Moscatelli, away from the communications routes between Piedmont and Lombardy while the Italo-German troops withdrew east of the Ticino River. Directed by Oberst Buch, commander of SS-Polizei-Regiment 15, the operation involved a *Kampfgruppe* of the Waffen-Grenadier Brigade der SS, consisting of about seven hundred men belonging to I./82 (led by Stubaf. Emilio Bianchi) and the II./82 (led by Ostubaf. Giorleo) and by a heavy-weapons detachment.

3. The second phase of the operation, designated Hochland Ost-West, which involved the eastern shore of Lake d'Orta.

4. Vincenzo Moscatelli (born in Novara on February 3, 1908; died in Borgosesia on October 31, 1981) was a Communist from the start. After having been abroad for many years, he returned to Italy in 1930 to organize clandestine action against fascism in Emilia Romagna. Arrested in 1931, he was sentenced to sixteen years and six months in prison. Freed in December 1935, he was again arrested in March 1937 and sentenced to another six months in jail in Vercelli. On July 26, 1943, the day after the fall of fascism, he resumed directing the anti-Fascist movement in Valsesia and, after September 8, busied himself with organizing armed bands against the German occupation forces and later against RSI units.

5. The Garibaldi assault brigades were, during the Italian Resistance, the partisan brigades that were predominantly linked to the Italian Communist Party. Within the military forces of the resistance movement, the Garibaldi brigades constituted the largest and best-organized group.

6. The II./82, commanded by Stubaf. Sergio Bianchi.

Chapter XIII

1. In reality, the GNR was officially created on September 8, 1943. On September 15, 1943, Mussolini gave the order over Radio Munich to reconstitute the Milizia Volontaria per la Sicurezza Nazionale (Volunteer Militia for National Security), which had previously been disbanded by the Badoglio government after July 25, 1943. On September 30, the commander of the Milizia, Renato Ricci, quickly gave orders to reconstitute the MVSN legions, and at the same time to begin forming new units with young recruits.

2. Alessandro Scano, *Legionario! Dalla Tagliamento alle SS italiane* (Genoa, Italy: Effepi Edizioni, 2005), 20.

3. After September 8, 1943, Vincenzo Moscatelli was busy gathering stragglers and organizing guerrilla warfare against the German forces. Arrested on October 29 by the Carabinieri upon request of the German authorities in Vercelli, he was quickly freed by his comrades and many fellow citizens who attacked the barracks. After having taken refuge on Mount Briasco, along with Eraldo Gastone, also called Ciro, he organized guerrilla actions with the "Gramsci" detachment. With the arrival of new volunteers, Ciro and Cino's band then became

the 6th Garibaldi Brigade.

4. Scano, *Legionario!*, 34–35.

5. Davide Scano, born in Turin on May 6, 1900. A volunteer in 1917 during the First World War. After the war he joined the Royal Carabinieri, attaining the rank of sergeant. At the same time, he joined the Fascist Action Squads, joining the Fascist Party and participating in the March on Rome. Because of his political activity, he was forced to resign. He volunteered for the war in Spain as well as for the African campaign. In 1940, he joined the antiaircraft militia as a volunteer as a second lieutenant, assigned to command a machine gun battery in Val Susa. He was later recalled into the army, was promoted to first lieutenant, and was assigned to the logistic services. He was sent to France with the IV Army, and after September 8, 1943, he was captured by the Germans. Sent to a prison camp in Germany, he was one of the first to join the RSI. He returned to Italy in spring 1944 as an officer in the Italian SS with the Degli Oddi Battalion. After the Anzio front collapsed, the unit was garrisoned in Lombardy, where, on April 25, 1945, Davide Scano was arrested by a band of independent partisans.

6. Scano, *Legionario!*, 35.

7. Ibid., 37.

8. Ibid., 44–45.

Chapter XIV

1. Giuliano Bortolotti, *Non per guardarmi ma per ricordare: Memorie di un volontario della Legione SS italiana* (Voghera, Italy: Libreria Bottazzi, 2007).

2. Ibid., 24.

3. Ibid., 26.

4. Ibid., 33–40.

5. Ibid., 43.

6. Ibid., 62.

7. Ibid., 64–65.

Chapter XV

1. Interview granted to Silvano Olmi, April 3, 2009.

2. Who according to some sources would end up after the war by becoming secretary of the Italian Communist Party in Portici, in the province of Naples.

3. Sergio Corbatti and Marco Nava, *Sentire-Pensare-Volere: Storia della Legione SS italiana* (Milan: Ritter Edizioni, 2001), 101: "An old and experienced soldier coming from the cavalry, with which he had participated in the Greek campaign; almost forty years old, he was more a father than a superior to the young volunteers."

4. Ibid., 101: "Until the beginning of the American offensive, patrol actions were the main activity carried out by the battalion; these were obscure but tough actions which wore down, depressed and tired the men, quickly reducing the men to a shadow of themselves because of the continuous drain of losses; however, the morale of the SS volunteers remained high, stimulated by the example of their German comrades and comforted by the moral valor of their presence in the combat area, ready to shed their blood to redeem the shame of the surrender and the lost war."

5. The riverbed of the Urcionio was later covered over and turned into a plaza with a memorial monument to paratroopers.

6. Corbatti and Nava, *Sentire-Pensare-Volere*, 299: "There were about a dozen SS wounded, among whom was Scharführer Pasquale Scarpellino, hit by a burst in the chest while he was trying to recover the body of a wounded officer. For valor shown, the SS NCO was recommended for the Silver Medal."

Chapter XVI

1. Extract from memoirs *In maniche di camicia*, March 4, 1993, edited by Giorgio Prandina.

2. Now the Polish city of Olstyn, in East Prussia.

3. Probably the camp at Münsingen, where Italian volunteers were collected after September 8, 1943.

4. Weimar.

Chapter XVII

1. On September 8, 1941, the Pinerolo division, commanded since the previous July by General Adolfo Infante, was deployed in Thessaly, where it had carried out bitter antipartisan operations. Following the armistice, the division refused to turn over its arms to the Germans and replied with gunfire when requested to hand over the airport at Larissa. Following the disbanding of other Italian divisions in the area (Casale, Forlì, Modena, and Piemonte), General Infante decided to move hits troops into the region of the Pindus Mountains, where he reached an agreement with the British military mission to collaborate with Greek partisans of the ELAS (the Greek Democratic National Army, led by the monarchists). The men of the Pinerolo were then split up among the various partisan formations. After a brief period of bloody clashes with the Germans, relations with ELAS became difficult, because the Communist partisans did not put much faith in these new allies, who had been brutal occupiers up until then, and in the end decided to disarm them. The Italian soldiers were then interned in camps in Grevenà in Macedonia, Neraida in Thessaly, and Karpenison in the Pindus. Living conditions in these camps were harsh, and several thousand Italian soldiers died due to sickness and malnutrition, or as a result of German sweeps.

BIBLIOGRAPHY

Primary sources

Public archives

Bundesarchiv Berlin Lichterfelde, Germany
Bundesarchiv-Militärarchiv Freiburg, Germany
US National Archives, Washington, DC
Vojensky Historicky Archiv Praga, Czech Republic

Period magazines and publications

Signal magazine, various editions and issues
Das Schwarze Korps magazine, various issues
Avanguardia magazine, weekly politico-literary publication of the Italian SS Legion, various issues

Secondary sources

Published works

Italian volunteers in the Waffen-SS

Bortolotti, Giuliano. *Non per guardarmi ma per ricordare: Memorie di un volontario della Legione SS italiana*. Voghera, Italy: Libreria Bottazzi, 2007.

Corbatti, Sergio, and Marco Nava. *Karstjäger! Guerrilglia e controguerriglia nell'OZAK, 1943–45*. Seregno, Italy: Associazione MADM-Brianza Viva, 2005.

Corbatti, Sergio, and Marco Nava. *Sentire-Pensare-Volere: Storia della Legione SS italiana*. Milan: Ritter Edizioni, 2001.

D'Auria, Francesco Paolo. *Einer von Millionen: Ferdinand, la mascotte della Leibstandarte*. Milan: Editrice Mursia, 2011.

Landwehr, Richard. *Italian Volunteers of the Waffen-SS*. Glendale, OR: Siegrunen, 1987.

Lazzero, Ricciotti. *Le SS italiane*. Milan: Rizzoli, 1982.

Scano, Alessandro. *Legionario! Dalla Tagliamento alle SS italiane*. Genoa, Italy: Effepi Edizioni, 2005.

Vassalli, Giuseppe. *Andenken, ricordo 29a Division Grenadier Waffen-SS*. Pinerolo, Italy: NovAntico Editrice, 2012.

SS units

Afiero, Massimiliano. *4.SS-Polizei Panzergrenadier-Division*. Afragola, Italy: Associazione Culturale Ritterkreuz, 2017.

Afiero, Massimiliano. *Leibstandarte SS Adolf Hitler, 1943–1945*. Afragola, Italy: Associazione Culturale Ritterkreuz, 2013.

Afiero, Massimiliano. *Waffen-SS in Guerra*. Vol. 3, *1944–1945*. Afragola, Italy: Associazione Culturale Ritterkreuz, 2011.

Afiero, Massimiliano. *Waffen-SS in Guerra*. Vol. 4, *1939–1945*. Afragola, Italy: Associazione Culturale Ritterkreuz, 2012.

Duprat, François. *Les campagnes de la Waffen-SS*. Paris: Les Sept Couleurs, 1973.

Landemer, Henri. *La Waffen-SS*. Paris: Balland, 1972.

Pencz, Rudolf. *For the Homeland: The History of the 31st Waffen-SS Volunteer Grenadier Division*. Solihull, UK: Helion, 2002.

Steiner, Felix. *Die Freiwilligen: Idee und Opfergang*. Göttingen, Germany: Plesse Verlag, 1958.

Trang, Charles. *Leibstandarte, 1943–45*. Bayeux, France: Editions Heimdal, 2008.

Second World War

Ahlfen, Hans von. *Der Kampf um Schlesien, 1944–1945*. Stuttgart: Motorbuch Verlag, 1991.

Baratter, Lorenzo. *Le Dolomiti del Terzo Reich*. Milan: Mursia, 2005.

Gentile, Carlo. *I crimini di guerra tedeschi in Italia, 1945–1945*. Turin, Italy: Einaudi, 2015.

Neulen, Hans Werner. *An Deutscher Seite*. Munich: Universitas, 1985.

Periodicals

Der Freiwillige magazine, various issues

La Legione magazine, quarterly magazine published by the Associazione d'Arma Fiamme Nere, issue 4, October–December 1999

Ritterkreuz magazine, bimonthly dedicated to Waffen-SS formations, various issues

Siegrunen magazine, periodical published by Richard Landwehr, various issues

Photographic references

Berlin Document Center (BDC)
Bundesarchiv, Germany (BA)
Deutsche Wochenschau films (DW)
Imperial War Museum (IWM)
Ljubljana Institute of Modern History (MZNS)
National Archives and Records Administration, Washington, DC (NA)

Private collections

Massimiliano Afiero (MA), Giorgio Bussano (GB), Archivo Corbatti (AC), Hubert Kuberski (HK)

Massimiliano Afiero was born in Afragola (Naples Province) in 1964. An information technology teacher and programmer, he has been interested in military history since his youth, specializing in the history of Axis units during the Second World War and particularly in the Waffen-SS. He has published numerous articles in the principal Italian-language history magazines and has contributed to many military history websites. He is one of the few Italian historical researchers to have personally interviewed many veterans of the Waffen-SS, publishing their previously unpublished stories. He has published numerous books dealing with foreign volunteers in the German armed forces during the Second World War. From November 2004 to December 2008 he was the historical consultant and technical director of the magazine *Volontari* (Marvia Edizioni). Since May 2008 he has been editor in chief of the bimonthly magazine *SGM* (*Seconda Guerra Mondiale*) published by Editoriale Lupo. In January 2009, he began publication of a new magazine, *Ritterkreuz*, dedicated to the military history of Axis units during the Second World War. Since 2013, he has also managed the publication of the Fronti di Guerra series, also dedicated to the Second World War.